L'art de la
SIMPLICITÉ

HOW TO LIVE MORE WITH LESS

Dominique Loreau

Copyright © Editions Robert Laffont 2011
English translation © Louise Rogers Lalaurie

This edition first published in Great Britain in 2016
by Orion
an imprint of the Orion Publishing Group Ltd
Carmelite House, 50 Victoria Embankment
London EC4Y 0DZ
An Hachette UK Company

7 9 10 8 6

A CIP catalogue record for this book
is available from the British Library.

ISBN: 978 1 4091 6385 5
TPB MMP ISBN: 978 1 4091 6386 2

Designed by carrdesignstudio.com
Printed in Great Britain by CPI Group (UK) Ltd, Croydon CR0 4YY

The Orion Publishing Group's policy is to use papers
that are natural, renewable and recyclable and made
from wood grown in sustainable forests. The logging and
manufacturing processes are expected to conform to the
environmental regulations of the country of origin.

Every effort has been made to fulfil requirements with regard to
reproducing copyright material. The author and publisher will be
glad to rectify any omissions at the earliest opportunity.

www.orionbooks.co.uk

Contents

For anyone in search of a simpler and better life, in mind, body or spirit, and at home: a helping hand to explore the vast potential that has been gifted to us all

Spring, in my cabin.
Utterly, wholly empty,
Utterly replete.

Haïku by Matsuo Bashō

Introduction

Growing up in France, but endlessly curious about the rest of the world, I determined to travel aboard in my student years. At nineteen, I worked as a classroom assistant in England, and at twenty-four I attended university in Missouri. I explored most of the other states of the Union, too, together with Canada, Mexico, and Central America. But when I visited the Japanese Tea Garden in San Francisco's Golden Gate Park, I felt an overpowering need to discover the true source of so much beauty. I travelled to Japan, a country I realised I had been drawn to forever, though I had never been able to put my yearning into words. I went to Japan, and stayed.

The experience of two such different civilisations provoked endless self-examination. I began to search for *the* perfect way of life. And by a gradual process of elimination, I came to understand that the pursuit of simplicity was the right way for me to live both comfortably and at peace with my conscience.

Why Japan? I'm often asked, when I tell people I've been living here for over thirty years. And like everyone who has made Japan their adopted home, I answer: Japan is a passion, a deep-seated need. I feel at ease here, and spellbound, even now, by the prospect of exciting new discoveries, day after day.

For years, I have been fascinated by Japanese Zen and its many manifestations – wash painting, temples, gardens, thermal springs, cooking, ikebana (flower arranging) and more.

I was fortunate, very early on, to meet a teacher of *sumi-e* (ink wash painting), and spent ten years learning not only the art itself, but also the very Japanese mindset that comes with it: an acceptance of whatever life brings, without the constant need to dissect, analyse and explain. Put simply, *sumi-e* is an expression of the Zen way of life.

I taught French at a Buddhist university, and spent time training as a novice nun at Aichi Senmon Niso-do Zen temple, in Nagoya. When I left, I understood better than ever how, beneath the country's modern, hi-tech veneer, this ancestral philosophy informs every aspect of Japanese life, down to the tiniest details. The better I came to know Japan, the more I understood the positive, enriching value of simplicity: a principle that classical philosophers, Christian mystics, Buddhists and Indian sages have striven to teach down the centuries, leaving us free to live unencumbered by prejudice, constraints and burdens that can disturb our focus and lead to stress. Simplicity offers the solution to so many problems.

Learning to live the simple life was no simple matter, however. I experienced a process of gradual metamorphosis, an increasingly urgent need to live with fewer things, but more lightness, freedom and fluidity; greater refinement, too. Little by little, I realised that, as I lightened my load, the things that were left seemed less and less vital. We actually need very little to live. And so I came to the unshakeable, profound conviction that the less we have, the greater our sense of freedom, and the better we are able to thrive.

I understood the need for caution, too: consumerism, inertia (both physical and mental), and negativity are waiting to ensnare us whenever our determination falters.

This book is the result of notes jotted throughout my years in Japan: it is the record and sum of my experiences and encounters, my reading and thinking, an expression of a personal ideal, a creed, a code of conduct, a way of life I aspire to continually, and work hard to implement. I keep all my notebooks, carrying them with me carefully wherever I go, as a kind of personal compass, reminding me of things I tend to forget, or fail to put into practice. They are a source of comfort, too, an affirmation of my most deeply held beliefs when, all around me, everything seems to be going awry. My notebooks are a precious storehouse of advice and exercises to dip into and practise as required, adaptable to new challenges, and to my changing needs, capabilities and circumstances. (You will find space to make your own notes on page 239.)

We are only just beginning to realise the dangers of excess and opulence. More and more people are seeking the joys and benefits of a simpler, more natural existence, looking beyond the endless temptations of consumerism to devise new, meaningful, contemporary lifestyles.

This book is for all those people.

My hope is that it will help promote a proper understanding of the art of simplicity as a truly fulfilling way of life.

PART I

MATERIALISM
AND
MINIMALISM

1

Material excess

Western society has lost the art of living simply. We have too many material possessions, too many temptations and desires, too much choice, too much to eat.

We waste and destroy so much. We use throwaway knives and forks, pens, lighters, cameras – and to make them we pollute our water and air, the landscape and nature. It's up to us to tackle waste here and now, before we find ourselves forced to confront the issue tomorrow.

Only once we have eliminated waste can we catch a glimpse of new possibilities ahead; only then can our everyday, essential activities – dressing, eating, sleeping – take on new meaning, a different and deeper dimension. We do not seek perfection, but a life more richly lived. Opulent luxury brings neither grace nor elegance. It imprisons and destroys the soul, while simplicity offers the solution to so many problems.

An excess of possessions leaves us no time to devote to our bodies. But when we feel comfortable in our own skin, we are free to cultivate our mind and spirit, better able to attain a happier and more meaningful existence.

Simplicity means possessing little, clearing the way for the bare necessities, the quintessence of things.

Simplicity is beautiful because it brings hidden joys.

The burden of possessions

THE NEED TO HOARD

Most of us journey through life with a great deal – often excessive amounts – of baggage. We should pause for thought and ask ourselves, why we are so attached to things?

For many people, material wealth is an expression of selfhood, proof of their existence. Consciously or otherwise, they associate their identity and self-image with the things they possess. The more they have, the more secure, accomplished and fulfilled they feel. Everything becomes objectified and aspirational: material goods, bargains, works of art, acquaintances, ideas, friends, lovers, holidays, a god, even the ego. People consume, acquire, accumulate, collect. They 'have' friends and contacts, 'hold' diplomas, titles, awards. They stagger under the weight of their possessions and forget, or fail to realise, that their acquisitiveness saps their vital energies, making them listless, and subject to increasingly urgent needs and desires.

Many things are superfluous, but we only realise this when they are gone. We used them because they were there, not because they were essential. How often do we buy things simply because we've seen them in someone else's home?

HOARDING AND INDECISION

'The world of relationships and acquaintances is rich enough
to fill our lives, without the need to add useless ornaments
that do nothing but encumber the spirit and our leisure time.'

Charlotte Périand, *A Life of Creation*

Making a simpler life means making sometimes difficult choices. Many people end their lives surrounded by literally tons of objects they feel no affection for, and which are of no use, because they have been unable to decide what to do with them, and lacked the courage either to sell them, or to give or throw them away. Such people remain anchored to the past, to their forebears, their memories, but they ignore the present and cannot envisage the future.

Throwing things away requires effort. Getting rid of things is not difficult in itself, but judging what is useful and what is not can be. Letting certain objects go can be extremely difficult, but your satisfaction will be all the greater.

FEAR OF CHANGE

'Respectable men who are well-to-do
Want you to think just like they do.'

Jake Thackray, 'The Scapegoat' (from Thackray's version of Georges
Brassens' song *'La mauvause réputation'*)

Our culture finds it hard to accommodate people who choose to live frugally: they constitute a threat to the economy, and to our consumer society. Such people find themselves marginalised, as individuals to be viewed with fear and suspicion. People who, by choice, live modestly, eat sparingly, waste little and never – or hardly ever – indulge in small talk, are generally thought of as mean, hypocritical, and antisocial. But to make that change is to embrace life. We are vessels, not commodities. Ridding ourselves of our possessions can help us become the man or woman we always wanted to be.

Many will object that they experienced hardship as children and see the process of material divestment as wasteful in itself. It makes them feel guilty. But this process is only wasteful if we throw away things we can still put to good use. If we rid ourselves of things that serve no purpose, we are not wasting anything. It is far more wasteful to hold on to something that's of no use to us: we waste our available space when we cram it full of things, and we waste energy trying to decorate our sitting room to match the photographs in interiors magazines. We waste time tidying things up, cleaning them, hunting for them.

Do memories make us happy? Objects are often said to have souls, but should our attachment to the things of the past clutter our future, or keep us trapped in the status quo?

CHOOSE THE MINIMUM

'A man is rich in proportion to the number of things which he can afford to let alone.'

Henry David Thoreau, *Walden*

Economy as a way of life is a practical philosophy, because living with little improves the quality of existence.

Things are not the embodiment of our inner being. To embrace minimalism we may need a degree of spiritual and intellectual baggage, rather than material possessions. Some cultures, such as Korea, are instinctively drawn to simplicity and understatement, as Korea's artistic tradition amply demonstrates.

We can all choose the riches that come with owning little. What matters is the courage to carry our convictions through. Discipline, clarity and determination are the preconditions for a life lived with the strict minimum, in clean, airy rooms. Minimalism requires an ordered lifestyle and careful attention to detail. Eliminate as much as possible, resist becoming overwhelmed by objects and items of furniture, then concentrate on what really matters, free of the constant concern that comes with clutter. Decisions will become natural and instinctive, your dress sense will be more elegant, your home more comfortable and your diary less crowded. Basic good sense will reassert itself. You will find yourself contemplating life with greater lucidity. Learn to eliminate quietly, carefully, but firmly and thoroughly.

Pause for a moment and think about what you can do to achieve a simpler, easier life. Ask yourself:

- What makes my life complicated?
- Is it worth it?
- When am I happiest?
- Is having more important than being?
- How far am I prepared to divest?

A tip: make lists – they will help you declutter your life.

USE AS LITTLE AS POSSIBLE

'[The] ability to live without furniture, without impedimenta,
with the least possible amount of neat clothing, shows more
than the advantage held [by the Japanese] in the struggle
of life; it shows also the real character of some weaknesses
in our own civilisation. It forces reflection upon the useless
multiplicity of our daily wants.'

Lafcadio Hearn, *Kokoro*

Pause in front of any object that catches your attention, and reflect on its gradual dissolution: it is crumbling slowly, and one day it will return to dust.

Nothing is more gratifying than knowing how to gauge, methodically and clear-sightedly, the true value of every object encountered in life: what is its practical use, what aspect of life does it belong to, how does it enhance your existence? Try to discern its constituent parts, their probable lifespan, and the feelings and sensations they inspire in you.

Do not enrich your life with objects. Instead, enrich your body with sensations, your heart with feelings, and your mind with principles.

Clearly, the only way to avoid being possessed by material things is to own nothing (or almost nothing) and, above all, to desire as little as possible. Accumulated possessions are a burden. Multiple, eclectic desires are also burdens.

Divest yourself of material things as you would remove an uncomfortable, chafing item of clothing. Only then can you reach your fullest potential.

—
13

We cannot be open and receptive if we have not made space first. Do not place material things above human values, above your own hard work and peace of mind, above beauty and freedom, or above living things in general.

An excess of things is invasive, overwhelming. It deflects our attention from the essentials. Our minds become cluttered, like an attic full of objects accumulated over time. We feel constrained, unable to move forward. But if we fail to move forward, we are not living. If we carry on accumulating possessions and pursuing multiple desires, we become confused, anxious and listless.

Think about how you feel when you pack the bare essentials into your car and set off for an unknown destination!

THE POSSESSOR IS POSSESSED

We do not possess things. We are possessed by things.

Each of us is free to have whatever we like, but what matters above all is our attitude to things, our knowledge of our own limits, needs and expectations: what we like to read, what films we enjoy, the places that make us profoundly happy.

A lipstick, some ID, a little money: the only three things a woman needs in a handbag. If you have only one nail file, you'll always know where to find it. Beyond basic comfort, a quality environment and one or two pieces of good furniture, material things should be of minimal importance. Refusing to own too much brings a greater appreciation of the things that give us spiritual, emotional and intellectual pleasure.

—
14

Throw away whatever is useless or worn out. (Or leave it on the street with a notice inviting anyone who can make use of it to help themselves.)

Give away useful items (books, clothing, dishes) to hostels or charities. The gesture will cost you nothing. On the contrary, you will feel a greater sense of satisfaction and well-being. Sell things you no longer (or rarely) use. Once you've made space, savour the privilege of having nothing that may prove attractive to thieves, mites or jealous minds. To own more than the strict minimum is to burden yourself with extra worries. And as everyone knows, throwing things overboard is the best way to stay afloat.

At home: say no to clutter

MAKE YOUR HOME A STRESS-FREE RETREAT

'Space and light and order. Those are the things that men need just as much as they need bread or a place to sleep.'

Le Corbusier

A home furnished with nothing but a handful of beautiful, absolutely essential things is a haven of peace. Cherish it, clean it and inhabit it with care and respect – it is a protective shell for your greatest treasure: your own self.

Only once we are free of material concerns can we truly thrive.

The body shelters our mind and spirit, and home shelters and nurtures our body. Only when the mind and spirit are free can they truly develop.

Each of our possessions should remind us we need nothing but the thing itself, that it is absolutely fit for purpose, that without it we would find it hard to 'function'.

Home should be a place of rest, a source of inspiration, a healing retreat. In our overpopulated, noisy cities, we feel distracted and assaulted by colour and variety. Home should be a place to replenish our energy reserves, and find new vitality, harmony and serenity. It should be a place of protection, both materially and psychologically, for body and spirit alike.

Malnutrition may be physical or spiritual. For the spiritually malnourished, home has its role to play. Our health depends on what we eat; what we choose to put in our home can have serious repercussions for our psychological well-being.

FLUIDITY, VERSATILITY, AND ZERO DECORATION

'It was this love of the abstract that led the Zen to prefer black and white sketches to the elaborately coloured paintings of the classic Buddhist School.'

Mai Mai Sze, *The Tao of Painting*

'Superfluidity' in an interior is the product of careful planning and choices. The result is an ideal space requiring minimum maintenance, tidying or other work: a space that delivers comfort, calm and *joie de vivre*.

Bauhaus, Shaker, and Japanese interiors are characterised by their shared focus on efficiency, flexibility and the concept of 'less is more'.

A plainly furnished home allows you to move around with ease. Objects and furnishings should be lightweight, aesthetically pleasing, and comfortable. The eye should detect the softness of a carpet, the scent of a wall treatment in aromatic wood, the cool, fresh feel of a shower space. Throw out cumbersome ashtrays, woollen rugs too heavy to move, lamps with leads that constantly snare the feet, fussy embroideries inherited from a beloved aunt, tarnished copper pots that never come clean, and the hundred other dust traps cluttering your chimney piece, dresser, sofa and shelves.

Focus on altering intrusive architectural details, installing functional, soft lighting, replacing faulty taps. Comfort is an art, and without it, any attempt at decoration will be in vain.

'Floating' architect-designed interiors – the epitome of 'white space' – are designed to allow objects to live and breathe thanks to the empty space around them. Devotees of the style make few compromises: a handful of books, a scented candle and a big, soft, good-quality sofa.

A room furnished with empty space draws in natural light and becomes filled with positive influences. Any object becomes a work of art; a minute of your time becomes a moment to treasure.

People who live in clean, empty spaces feel in control of their lives. They are not 'possessed', and feel a greater satisfaction and comfort as a result.

There is no beauty without empty space. There is no music without silence. Everything takes on meaning and significance. In a plain, minimalist interior a cup of tea, a book, or the face of a friend on Skype asserts tremendous presence. In an empty space, everything becomes a composition, a still life, a picture.

The Bauhaus movement's first houses were much criticised for their austere appearance, despite their undeniable beauty. But they were models of functionality and common sense, even temples of the senses, with spaces set aside for sun-lounging, bathing and personal care. Everything was carefully planned for comfort and practicality.

SLIM YOUR HOME

Simplify your interior by creating one large space (for example) from three small rooms. Ridding yourself of useless objects delivers the same sense of well-being as natural, whole foods after a diet of industrially produced ready meals.

Eliminate whatever is not working perfectly. Ask an electrician to help you run wires and leads behind skirting boards, under parquet floors or in concealing strips. Change faulty taps, noisy flushes, cramped shower cubicles, awkward door handles – the many tiny annoyances that pollute our everyday lives.

One of the great advantages of our time is the miniaturisation of our means of communication, so that we need less and less space in which to work.

Decoration is unimportant in a home – what matters are the people who live there. Quality materials are the key to comfort. Choose them with your eyes closed. Remember that cashmere is not a luxury for the wealthy: a pashmina shawl will keep you warmer in bed than two cheap blankets, adapts to any room in the house, and can be carried in your car or onto a plane. It is beautiful, wonderfully soft, and lasts for years.

Choose monochrome over colour. Colour can be tiring to the eye: white, black and grey are the absence of colour and the fusion of all colours. They offer the essence of simple style, as if life's complexities had been eliminated by a process of distillation.

YOU ARE THE SPACE YOU INHABIT

When we take possession of a new living space, we try it on like a new coat, see how well it fits our personality, and settle into it like a protective carapace, a cocoon.

Often, the things we choose to communicate to the outside

world reflect our innermost sense of self. Yet many people remain undecided as to their personal tastes, unsure of what brings them true satisfaction.

Creating an environment that matches our deepest aspirations enables us consciously to orchestrate the existing link between our inner and outer selves.

Architects and ethno-sociologists agree that our living space makes us who we are, that a home shapes the mind and spirit of the people who live in it.

Our environment trains our personality and influences the choices we make. Our understanding of a person deepens once we have visited their home.

Home should not be a source of worry or additional work; it should not be a burden. On the contrary, it should be a place in which to replenish our inner resources.

'Clutter' has the same root as 'clot'. Just as a blood clot blocks the circulation, so clutter can disrupt the proper functioning of an interior.

Too many homes look like bric-a-brac shops or furniture store-rooms. In a traditional Japanese interior a room is only 'lived in' when it is physically occupied. When a person leaves a room, they leave no trace of their existence or activities. All practical items (futon beds, ironing boards, work desks, occasional tables, floor cushions) are compact, or designed to be folded away, so that they can be stowed out of sight after use

Rooms like these allow their occupants to move freely, undisturbed by the memory of other presences, from this world or any other.

A MINIMAL HOME

Make your home compact, comfortable, practical.

Living with ease is your ultimate goal. Often, comfort depends on space. Adequate space, liberating space, generous space. Living in 'condensed' mode can be a virtue.

Partly from necessity, partly due to their religious beliefs and ethics, Japanese people have long cultivated an aesthetic of the 'absolute': each tiny detail is important. When even the smallest space is perfectly arranged, we forget its size.

A small, perfect space, a good book and a cup of tea are a source of extreme satisfaction.

Living with very little is an ideal, demanding a specific state of mind: choose empty space over opulence, silence over cacophony, classic, long-lasting pieces over the latest must-have furnishings. Ultimately, your aim is to create enough space to move freely. Eliminate the many, often unnoticed, obstacles that make you feel cramped and confined. A plain, empty space can be cosy and welcoming if it is treated with warm, natural textiles and 'soft' materials such as wood, cork or straw.

There is more space in a big travel trunk containing a few absolute necessities than in a huge building crammed with things that are never used but 'may come in handy one day'. Remember this when you furnish your home.

Times change, and so should we, as we adapt to new ideas and lifestyles. With more and more of the world's population living in increasingly crowded cities, many people find themselves occupying smaller apartments. We will do well to follow the Japanese example, and learn to live beautifully, quietly and contentedly in less space.

The private boudoir, so beloved of nineteenth-century ladies, could make a timely comeback today. A washbasin, a hanging rail, a mirrored wall, a small sofa for resting and reading – in short, a private space in which to recharge and take care of oneself, in comfort and peace. A boudoir is the perfect complement to a modern bathroom, designed for easy bathing or showering, but where everything else (applying make-up, dressing, undressing, pedicures, depilation, etc.) is awkward and uncomfortable.

A few square metres, better used, can work miracles.

AN EMPTY ROOM

A seemingly empty room can be truly luxurious if it is carefully designed, with attention to detail. An empty space allows its occupants to clear their thoughts, as in the vestibule of a grand hotel, a church or a temple. Architectural design in the 1950s followed the same principle, with its emphasis on straight lines and sheer chrome surfaces. The resulting interiors are not empty and void; rather, they exude a sense of quiet and order. Simplification is a means of embellishment. Embellishment 'to point zero' is the ideal way to reduce stress.

Yes, minimalism can be costly. A scattering of ornaments may be cheaper than a plain wall panel in fine wood. But a minimalist lifestyle needs more than cash. It demands unshakeable conviction. A life dedicated to order and beauty can be achieved without neglecting your passions: music, yoga, collecting, hi-tech gadgetry. Never treat something you consider a personal talisman as you would a simple, decorative piece, however. Your talisman is your personal energy source, and should be kept in its own special place.

Try an experiment, just for one week: put all your ornaments away, out of sight. The empty space will be a revelation.

Remember: living in the past, for memories alone, means over-looking the present and closing the doors to the future.

A BEAUTIFUL, HEALTHY HOME

The things we have around us speak to us. If we settle for cheap or poor design, we pay the price. Paying careful attention to the aesthetic beauty of our surroundings refines our sensibility. The greater our attention to detail, the more our surroundings nurture us. Once we've tried dimmable lights, a switch that's either on or off, dazzling a room or plunging it into darkness, seems cruel and harsh. Anything in an interior that is not absolutely fit for purpose becomes a minor irritation, like a slight but nagging headache or toothache. Cupboards crammed with clothes (but nothing we can wear), piles of books (but nothing to read), a refrigerator full of out-of-date food, a freezer more ice-bound than the North Pole, are all symptoms of an 'unhealthy' home. Built-in cupboards, light sources set into the ceiling or walls, and an absence of clutter are the key to a restful interior with room to breathe and focus on essentials. Never compromise; never hold on to useless things.

ENERGISE YOUR INTERIOR

'Perfumes, colours and sounds answer one another.'

Baudelaire

The Chinese have practised feng shui (the science of the transmission of energy) in their homes for five thousand years. Chinese people believe that we are permanently influenced by the world around us (the weather, people with whom we come into contact, objects etc.), and that consciously or unconsciously the things that fill our everyday lives have the power to delight or irritate us every day, all the time.

We ourselves have the capacity to influence the world around us, by our attitudes, and by the way we walk, talk and behave. Our vibrations and energy act upon living things, and can affect our material surroundings. We receive and transmit the life energy known as 'qi'.

Cleanliness is paramount in feng shui. If a room is well ordered and cared for, the lives of the people who use it will be the same: the mind feels more lucid, decision-making becomes more clear-cut.

The entrance to your home should be welcoming and bright, with flowers: the elements concentrated here will suffuse the rest of your interior. Brighten a small, dark hallway with a mirror, or a brightly coloured painting. Qi should circulate freely throughout the home, with no obstructions.

Your home is nourished by the things you allow or invite into it. Every object placed in the entrance will multiply its impact on your interior. The colours in your entrance will radiate their innate energy and leave their imprint on the qi.

Corners deflect and fragment the qi. Soften them with round-leafed houseplants: this will transform the atmosphere of an entire room.

Sounds, colours, materials and plants should enrich your interior with their own subtle vibrations. Our world needs to function in perfect harmony with the laws of the universe. Observing and understanding the foundations of life enables us to tune in and consciously incorporate universal laws into our existence, so that we are no longer swimming against the current.

Ensure abundance and plenty by keeping your home well stocked with food and provisions, and storing them all in one place. Never allow supplies to run low – this will create a sense of hardship and need. Your fruit bowl should always be full, and your refrigerator free of wilting vegetables and three-day-old leftovers. Sharp, trenchant objects (knives, scissors) should be kept out of sight, and ailing houseplants or wilting flowers should be thrown away (watching the slow death of plants is subconsciously very depressing). Chinese people never eat reheated leftovers and only cook with the freshest of ingredients. They understand the importance of this for their energy reserves.

Chinese people also believe that dried flowers in a room will absorb vital energies in order to revive themselves; that a waste bin in the wrong place (near a tap) will affect the quality of the water with bad vibrations (the art of water divining supports this theory).

Keeping your apartment clean, bright and free of negative qi will transform the image you communicate to others, even when you are far away from home. Stay in harmony with your interior, wherever you are. A clean, neat house when you set out for work in the morning, will transform your day!

Qi is affected by the raw material and form of each object it passes. Dust and dirt are traps for stagnant qi, destroying the harmony and balance in your home. Fitted carpet or rugs are material 'anchors': they magnify basic, existential resources. Energy rises from the floor, hence every surface in the home, and your shoes, should be clean. Oriental people always remove their shoes when entering a home.

Feng shui achieves maximum impact once we have identified our essential, inner being; when we live every moment of our lives in harmony with our innermost, profound nature, our true selves.

SOUND AND LIGHT

'Moonlight is sculpture; sunlight is painting.'

Nathaniel Hawthorne, *American Notebooks*, 1838.

Light is life. When a person is deprived of natural light, they may fall ill or lose their sanity.

Avoid uniform lighting in your home. Natural light is constantly changing, subtly altering our perspective on whatever we see around us.

The 'soundscape' of home affects us, too, far more than we may realise: a creaking door, a sudden, loud ringtone. But hinges can be oiled, music can announce an incoming call, and fitted carpet can do much to soften intrusive noise.

When buying household appliances, always choose the quietest models. The human ear readily accepts a conversation at 60 decibels, but suffers any noise louder than 120. A food mixer functioning at 100 decibels is a nuisance. Choose your ringtones, alarms and doorbells with care.

SPACE FOR STORAGE

'Good storage should be structured according to our range of movements, movements which are dictated by our needs. The essential element of household facilities is storage. Without storage, there cannot be empty space in the home.'

Charlotte Perriand, *A Life of Creation*

A house is home not only to its human occupants, but also to a host of things, and sometimes animals, too. As such, every home needs enough built-in storage to avoid mess and the unplanned build-up of free-standing cupboards, chests of drawers, trunks and myriad ill-assorted objects.

Rather than plain, empty cupboards, storage space should be planned and fitted out for specific needs. You shouldn't have to stand on a stool every time you need to fetch a cooking pot, nor should you have to cross the kitchen to put away a teaspoon after washing up. Things become scattered and untidy because they lack practical storage space in which to 'live'.

Storage and cupboards should be placed in or close to the space in which their contents are used: this will minimise repetitive movements and footfall for the house's occupants. Each floor in the house should have its own cleaning cupboard, for example. The food larder should be near the kitchen; towels and nightclothes should be kept in a cupboard near the bathroom, and a 'cloakroom' space should be installed near the front door, for outdoor clothes, bags, umbrellas, shoes and visitors' luggage. Why are these spaces so seldom taken into account by architects planning a new apartment block?

A rational approach to the design of efficient living spaces is the key to productive work, rest and well-being.

Things: what should stay, and what should go?

MUST HAVES

What are our essential needs? Just whatever we need to live, and then, enough to live well.

Throughout the Middle Ages, material minimalism and spirituality went hand in hand. Prior to the Renaissance, medieval clothing, food, and homes were designed to answer reasonable needs, nothing more. But in today's world, enough is never enough.

A well-known photographer reported that having investigated individual possessions around the world, Mongolians were found to own around 300 objects each, while Japanese people owned around 6,000 items.

How many things do you own?

How do we define the 'minimum'?

A table, a bed and a candle in a monastery or prison cell are one (admittedly bare and depressing) example. To live *well*, we need to add just two or three other, beautiful things, depending on the extent of our ascetic inclinations: things chosen carefully to nourish the soul and satisfy our craving for beauty, our need for comfort and security. One fine gemstone, an Italian sofa . . .

The ideal: to live with the strict minimum, in a dream setting, with an impeccable interior and a well-honed, supple, perfectly groomed body. And to be absolutely independent, leaving the mind clear and open to a world of new discoveries.

The most basic human needs are, first, to live in conditions that allow us to maintain our health, equilibrium and dignity; and second, to have access to quality clothing, food and surroundings. Sadly, in today's world, even quality of life has become a luxury.

PERSONAL POSSESSIONS

A person's intimate possessions should fit into a couple of suitcases: a well-chosen capsule wardrobe, a vanity case, an album of favourite photographs, two or three treasured objects. The rest – the objects that fill our homes (bedlinen, dishes, TV, furniture) – are not 'personal' possessions in the strictest sense.

Adapting your lifestyle to this end brings serenity and peace of mind. You will gain what few possess: an open, receptive state of mind.

Think about your exit from this world as early as possible in life: leave a house, a car, some money . . . and a handful of treasured memories. No silver spoons, no knick-knacks, no inheritance issues, no intimate journal.

Throw out your gadgets, and tell everyone around you what you plan to do. Swap your battered armchairs for a really comfortable, good-quality sofa, your silver for impeccable, stainless steel, dresses you no longer wear for a soft, expensive cardigan, your network of acquaintances for a few, true friends, and your therapy sessions for a case of fine champagne!

What remains are mystery and beauty, the things of the intellect, the mind, and the emotions. Reorganise your life for a simpler, brighter, livelier existence. And persuade your life partner to do the same.

Say no to inertia and accumulation, sad songs and glum people; they are dead weights that cause us to pile up layer upon layer of false values and habits, burdens that blind us to reality and prevent us from focusing on the unexploited resources of our minds, hearts, and imaginations.

THINK 'LITTLE', LIVE 'LIGHT' AND SIMPLY

'It is desirable that a man ... live in all respects so compactly and preparedly that, if an enemy take the town, he can ... walk out the gate empty-handed without anxiety.'

Henry David Thoreau, *Walden*

Remain alert and ready to face the unexpected.

Make a detailed, personal list of all your possessions. This will help you to strip out things that are of no use. With the exception of a few flights of fancy in your wardrobe, your possessions should be kept to the strict minimum, and able to be carried by you and you alone. Historically, Japanese people were forced to live like this because of the prevalence of fire, bandits and natural disasters. They chose things they could carry with them if they were forced to take flight.

Do not acquire material possessions, and ensure that whatever you do own is essential, practical and fit for purpose. Remember, weight is your enemy: weight is not good for objects, nor is it good for your health. The greater the travellers, the lighter their baggage.

Try to replace your possessions with others that are smaller and more lightweight. Sell your oak cupboards and chests and opt for cleverly fitted, built-in storage.

Think of your bedroom as an alcove, or your house as a small boat. Remember that the finest Moroccan *dar* may be furnished with nothing but a scattering of rugs, cushions, and folding brass tray tables. Cumbersome pieces of furniture weigh as heavily on the consciousness as they do on the shoulders of whoever has to move them. They restrict ease of movement around a room (unless your home is a palace).

Whether you are looking for a set of beautiful wood shelves or a tea bowl, a kitchen table or a wallet, try to find items best suited to your personal use and handling. They will encourage greater fluidity of movement.

Remember: when you live with the strict minimum, every item, no matter how small, must be both functional and beautiful.

A home is like a travel case: both contain our most personal possessions – our own selves, eternal nomads.

THE ESSENCE OF THINGS

Things must be left to ripen before we can extract their quintessence.

Make a point of defining, describing, looking at, naming, evaluating, and experiencing the objects in your life. It will help you become aware of what is superfluous. Look closely at the fine detail of things: their true quality and value (or their mediocrity and lack of utility) will become clear. Look beyond their superficial appearance, to see what they actually contribute to your existence. 'Essential' experiences and objects have a universal quality: a star glimpsed through the morning mist, a dazzling ray of sunshine, a teapot that looks like a teapot, not like an elephant – the sort of teapot a child might draw for you.

But remember: the simplest objects should be of the finest quality.

DON'T SUFFER YOUR POSSESSIONS, CHOOSE THEM

'The old painter Wang-Fo and his disciple were wandering along the roads of the Kingdom of Han. They made slow progress because Wang-Fo would stop at night to watch the stars, and during the day to watch the dragonflies. They carried hardly any luggage because Wang-Fo loved the image of things, and not the things themselves, and no object in the world seemed to him worth buying except brushes, pots of lacquer and China ink, and rolls of silk and rice paper.'

Marguerite Yourcenar, *Oriental Tales* (tr. Alberto Manguel)

Appreciate owning very little.

No one can own every shell in the sea. And seashells are so much more beautiful in isolation! We cannot appreciate great hordes of objects: they lose their essential soul and beauty. They are 'dead'.

The Japanese understand this. Since ancient times, they have mastered the art of surrounding themselves with small, unostentatious things: things that speak to their owner, not the mass of people, things that bridge the psychological gulf between themselves and their owner. Each object is well made, aesthetic, useful, compact, lightweight, foldable, mobile, and has the power to disappear before and after use, into a bag, a pocket, or beautifully folded in a silk square. Objects are appreciated when they are in use, and respected as sacred items in their own right. Children are taught about this very strictly.

If we are to age better, to tread more lightly as we go forward, we should take inspiration from the Japanese and their customs, and adopt a lifestyle focused on strict essentials, but embracing comfort and refinement.

The universal over-incursion of technology into our lives diminishes the life of the spirit. We are content with mediocre things. But if we focus solely on our vital needs and innermost desires, we will surround ourselves only with things of the finest quality.

Learn to know yourself. Learn how to define and express your tastes, and the things you dislike. If you see the garden of your dreams, try to define and express exactly how it looks, how it feels. If it is green and 'clean', don't plant your own garden with beds of yellow tulips on one side, and pink geraniums on the other. A garden of varied foliage is restful to the eye. Repetitive floral borders and tubs are an insult to nature. Too many different plants cohabiting in a small courtyard or garden will look artificial and cluttered.

Material possessions should serve the body, or nourish the soul. Be rigorously selective, your quality of life will improve as a result. If our senses and nutrition are nourishment enough, then anything else is excess and, like too much food, will have a detrimental effect.

First, identify the things best suited to you, the things you love best of all (in clothes, furniture, cars). Labels, brand names and packaging are of no importance.

Train yourself to evaluate the objects around you. Your peace of mind will grow as, gradually, the things that make up your everyday world come to reflect your true needs and personal tastes.

ACCEPT INTO YOUR WORLD ONLY WHATEVER SATISFIES YOUR SENSES

'The key to loving how you live is in knowing what it is you truly love.'

Sarah Ban Breathnach

Thoughts count, but so do things. Most people never succeed in identifying precisely the things they really love, the things that best suit their lifestyle.

Objects are the recipients of our emotions. They should be both practical and a source of pleasure. Identify and reject anything that seems ugly or out of place: its negative energy will affect your well-being as surely as noise pollution, or a poor diet.

Living permanently with objects we dislike makes us apathetic and miserable. When objects irritate us (consciously or otherwise), they provoke toxic hormonal secretions. How often do we say, 'That's poison, it's so irritating, it kills me . . .'? But a perfect object is a source of unparalleled comfort, security and serenity.

Promise yourself to keep only the things you love. The rest is meaningless. Don't let your world become filled by the past, or by objects you find mediocre. Own little, but the best of everything. Don't settle for a 'good enough' armchair. Buy the most beautiful, lightweight, ergonomic and comfortable armchair you can afford.

—

Don't hesitate to discard things that are 'more or less OK'. Replace them with objects that are perfect and fit for purpose, even if this means spending what many will dismiss as wasteful sums of money. Minimalism can be costly: contentment with the strict minimum comes at a price.

Your mistakes are your guide. By choosing the wrong thing, you can identify what's perfect for you.

CHOOSE THINGS THAT ARE PRACTICAL, ROBUST, ERGONOMIC AND MULTI-FUNCTIONAL

'Form and function are one.'

Frank Lloyd Wright

Simplicity is the perfect union of the beautiful, useful and appropriate. Nothing should be superfluous.

Own only a small number of things, either artisan-made or mass-produced, but be careful to select them as extensions of yourself: objects are our servants, not our masters. If a jug corresponds perfectly to the shape and movement of your hand, you will use it more often than if your wrist feels uncomfortable picking it up and pouring with it. A plain, transparent glass allows the eye to see straight away what it contains, and how much.

An object reveals its true value and quality in use. Don't try to find the objective 'best' at any price, look instead for reliable, long-lasting pieces that are perfectly suited to their purpose and your needs. Before making a purchase, touch the object, feel its heft and weight, open it, close it, screw it, unscrew it, test it, check it, ask to see or hear it (the sound of an alarm clock, a doorbell).

Ceramics should be lightweight; glassware should be strong. Yanagi Sōetsu, the Japanese philosopher and collector of folk art, reminds us that just as a good worker is strong and healthy, so an object destined for daily use should be robust and made to last. Finely decorated, delicate items are not for everyday use. If you want to see fine tableware, eat out at a chic restaurant from time to time, but buy thick, white, unbreakable, classic plates for yourself. They will match everything and make your food look appetising. Only people with eccentric tastes will find their plain elegance boring. Korean Yi Dynasty bowls, now costly and sought after, were originally humble rice vessels, not made to flatter the eye, but in response to the necessities of everyday life.

Everyday objects cannot be fragile or of poor quality; their practicality and beauty go hand in hand. Unusable objects have an aura of negativity, however beautiful they may be.

If we dread breaking an object because it is valuable, our fear spoils the pleasure we have in owning it and using it. The great Zen masters choose their personal treasures from everyday items and natural, unexceptional objects. In this way, they seek out beauty in its most unusual forms. True beauty is all around us. We don't see it because we look too far into the distance.

Even the most everyday things – a teapot or a knife – become beautiful when they are used regularly and appreciated for their practicality. They enrich our daily lives with small satisfactions that we alone can savour.

Cultivate a love of visual beauty rather than the perceived

—

'beauty' of a luxury label or logo. Surround yourself only with things answering your immediate needs, things whose beauty was not created for its own sake.

CHOOSE QUALITY BASICS THAT AGE WELL

Surround yourself with 'basics'. Free your imagination by choosing pieces manufactured according to artisan traditions drawing on the know-how, experience and wisdom of craftspeople who have handed down their techniques from generation to generation. Prefer these to the creations of individual artists, often made solely to boost their own reputations and personal wealth. Buying a quality bag or a string of pearls from a good jeweller may seem snobbish, but the cost and quality of the pieces are justified when you know how much work and skill have gone into their making. Choose the finest natural materials and shun superficial bling: the pure, serene white ceramics, or stone; expensive, beautifully smooth and glossy lacquerware; wood with a naturally beautiful grain; textiles that reveal their natural beauty (wool, cotton, silk). When we buy such things, we are buying a piece of ourselves.

With industrialisation, we have lost the ability to see and judge the intrinsic quality of an object. If you can't yet afford the sofa of your dreams, save for it little by little until you can. But don't buy a cheap substitute while you wait. You may find yourself becoming accustomed to it, at your cost!

It is better to live with high aspirations than mediocre realities.

Quality cannot be measured in monetary value. Quality is a response to the needs of an organism and its surroundings.

A quality object will embellish its surroundings with grace and elegance. Fine leather acquires a patina over time, becoming softer and glossier. A good tweed jacket must be broken in: it delivers more satisfaction and comfort with wear. Wood looks and feels warmer to the eye and heart the longer it is left to age. When a synthetic object ages, it becomes uglier and more irritating. Choose living materials.

QUALITY AND LUXURY

Too many objects 'kill' the impact of each one. An over-stimulating interior fetters the imagination, while simple things release it.

A harmonious colour scheme, and fine, natural materials in our everyday surroundings are soothing to the eye and touch: choose the natural grain and patina of wood, shaped by human hand but otherwise untainted.

Once you have savoured quality, you will never settle for mediocrity. But we are exposed to quality less and less frequently in today's consumer society, so that we no longer desire it (quality is expensive: it cannot be mass-produced, this is the definition of luxury).

As a store assistant selling leather goods once told me, a series of small, inexpensive things can cost more than a single, very fine purchase: the price may seem exorbitant, but the piece will give satisfaction for the rest of your life, and pleasure every time you use it.

THE ART OF HARMONISING

Owning one or two beautiful things is not enough. They should harmonise and reflect a single style, forming a coherent whole.

A style that reflects your personality will give the best impression of you.

Simplicity means creating harmony among very few objects, each one of which is unique and indispensable.

Add value and style to your life with economy and simplicity.

Often, in aesthetics as in so many other things, less is more. An object is beautiful when it is beautifully displayed, in isolation, but in harmony with its surroundings. A single bud in a vase encapsulates the natural world, the seasons, the mutability of things . . .

A teapot without cups, cups without a tray, a tray that clashes with the style of the room in which it is used, will shatter the harmony and serenity of a particular setting, at a particular moment. A large, rustic Louis XV cupboard will be out of place in a modern apartment.

Surround your objects with space and respect. Make the best use of the few things you have. A shelf crammed with porcelain figurines will not make your sitting room any more comfortable or elegant.

Purely decorative objects can make a room feel static, frozen, lifeless. Minimalism leaves space for the imagination, creativity and change.

A tip: when all the objects in an ensemble are the same colour, they seem fewer, are restful to the eye and create a sense of order.

Your wardrobe: simplicity with style

STYLE AND SIMPLICITY

'When a girl feels that she's perfectly groomed and dressed she can forget that part of her. That's charm. The more parts of yourself you can afford to forget the more charm you have.'

Scott Fitzgerald, 'Bernice Bobs her Hair' (short story)

Style is the outer garb of our inner thoughts. True personal style says 'no' to the eccentricities of fashion. It is the perfect marriage of what we wear and what we are.

'Fashion changes, but style endures.' So said Coco Chanel. Fashion is a permanent show, style is all about simplicity, beauty and elegance. Fashion can be bought; style is innate.

Style is a gift.

A woman's style should become plainer and simpler with age. Style creates presence; the true value of quality is the serenity it confers.

The ideal: wear your own reality, not clothes. Simplicity is the key to a distinctive, eye-catching appearance. This is as true for a woman as it is for a photograph, a polished wooden floor gleaming before an open fire, or a coffee table left bare except for two or three perfect, simple bowls. The same principle applies to architecture, poetry, and clothes.

An elegant woman avoids the 'Christmas tree' look. Simple, well-cut ensembles are perfect for day wear, and simple, graceful dresses for evening, accessorised with one or two fine pieces of jewellery. Elegant women allow themselves to be looked at and admired: they deserve and enjoy the attention.

As for colour: beige, grey, white and (of course) black are all you need.

It's said that women who wear black lead colourful lives. Explaining his passion for black, the great Japanese couturier Yohji Yamamoto points out that bright colours are disturbing to other people: they are disruptive and serve no purpose. Black and white are perfection, the essence of beauty, leaving us free to concentrate on what really matters: a person's skin tone, the colour of their hair or eyes, a fine piece of jewellery. All are enhanced most effectively by black or white, and sometimes navy blue or beige. As a general rule, avoid multicoloured, floral prints, spots or stripes.

The smart way to vary your wardrobe is to limit your palette: two or three different shades suffice, enlivened with careful touches of bold colour.

A plain, classic wardrobe makes it far easier to choose what to wear each morning, and cuts out the tedious chore of sorting and discarding unworn items. A dozen outfits that can be mixed and matched are enough to cover every occasion.

Clothes that are too tight or too loose-fitting are never elegant. Women become weary of the daily struggle to find clothes that suit them, which look elegant but also feel comfortable and attractive, so discard anything that doesn't coordinate with the rest of your wardrobe, anything that's too small, too old or surplus to requirements. Wearing worn-out clothes is very ageing. Make your wardrobe a haven of well-ordered peace. And if you don't need to 'dress' for work or to go out, buy two or three really good pairs of jeans – the absolute best solution for comfort, practicality and quality.

A well-dressed woman shows taste but also intelligence, wit and audacity.

Stay true to one distinctive style: if you strive to look like too many other people, you may lose sight of yourself. Know yourself, and your style will follow naturally.

Each day offers a succession of choices that can help us define our unique personality and style. Ideally, your choices will be based on your self-image, and the image you wish to project to others. In reality, the image you communicate right now is the sum of every detail of your daily life.

Style, a style, our style makes us feel comfortable in our own skin. Remember those moments in life when you have felt perfectly groomed and dressed, elegant and confident. Your feelings will have communicated themselves to everyone around you. Our choice of clothes and jewellery is a source of pleasure for other people, too. We have a duty to bring a touch of beauty to the world we live in. Each item in your wardrobe should exert its own presence. Create your own style.

DO YOUR CLOTHES SPEAK YOUR LANGUAGE?

Clothes are to the body what the body is to the mind. They should reflect our inner selves, look fetching and be perfectly functional, too. Start by planning your wardrobe in your head. Begin with accessories (shoes and bags) that reflect your personal style. Then take time to organise a proper wardrobe space of your own. Your clothes express what you are, what you want to be, your imagination, your determination, your standards, your politics, your dreams and your way of life. They speak volumes about you, before you say a word.

Life is not simple. We are all called upon to play a variety of roles. Who have you been today?

Our clothes become us; they take on the imprint of our personality. They are the overture to our conversations with our reflection in the mirror, our family, our entourage, everyone we encounter as we go about our lives. A wardrobe should reflect the quintessence of your personal style.

'Feeling comfortable in your own skin' is a meaningful phrase. The spirit of an item of clothing enters the body when it is worn. If we take life simply, as it comes, we will be free from excess.

Dressing well is a source of inner peace. It shows consideration for the self. When we dress our body to reflect our inner soul, we feel an immediate sense of harmony. Our clothes can be our friends, or our enemies. They can show us off to our best advantage, protect us, or communicate a false image of ourselves. They even have the magical power to change our behaviour.

SIMPLIFY YOUR WARDROBE

What clothes do you possess? What clothes do you need? Well-being depends on simplicity, good sense and harmony. The value of a piece of clothing lies in its simplicity. Once again, less is more.

Choose classic styles – pieces that can be worn for eight months of the year, whether single outfits or separates. Mix textures (velvet, leather, silk, wool or cashmere) for a bold, inventive look. Sort through your wardrobe: keep only the things you really love. It's never too late to become someone different: take a step in that direction today. Throw out items that don't suit you, or are old, anything you've scarcely worn, for whatever reason (or none). You'll be casting off all those pipe dreams and wrong-headed purchases, all those impulse buys made in moments of frustration or weakness.

Finding the ideal outfit eliminates the constant stress of feeling uncomfortable with what you wear. With the ideal outfit, you'll leave home in the morning feeling light-footed and good-humoured: one less thing to poison your existence.

'Less' means ridding yourself of those moments of hesitation in front of a wardrobe full of clothes that are 'more or less OK' or 'not too bad'. The items left after a thorough purge have more presence and value, and will be easier to coordinate. Staring at a dress you detest, hanging in your wardrobe day after day, is far more harmful than getting rid of it once and for all.

Every woman has made a wrong purchase that spoiled her natural elegance.

Unattractive clothes make us eat to compensate for our feelings of awkwardness. We wear 20 per cent of our wardrobe 80 per cent of the time. The rest is either unflattering, uncomfortable or worn out.

Don't keep clothes that don't look good on you right now. If you lose ten kilos, you'll want to refresh your wardrobe, too. Look at each garment afresh: think about how to accessorise it (with different tights, an unusual belt or beads). Don't wear an office skirt with a sweatshirt, or sports shoes with a formal handbag. Think about your different activities, and the outfits you need: make a list of what's missing.

WHAT YOU NEED

The only answer: 'real' clothes. Throw out anything that falls out of fashion from one season to the next.

An item of clothing should be good enough to withstand dozens of washes without ever going out of shape or bobbling.

Make sure you have a few key pieces (fine wool trousers, a tweed jacket for winter, and one or two in linen for summer, late spring and early autumn, one very good, very beautiful coat), and a variety of T-shirts and tops. Make sure you have at least three perfect outfits adaptable to all occasions (weekends, going out, work). If you spend a lot of time at home, put together a wardrobe that reflects this. Ask yourself, if you lost your suitcase – as I did when flying to California – what clothes would you buy?

The following wardrobe is all you need for several months of wear:

- 7 outdoor pieces (jackets, a raincoat, a coat)
- 7 tops (sweaters or polo necks, T-shirts, shirts)
- 7 other items (trousers, jeans, skirts, dresses)
- 7 pairs of shoes (for walking, ankle boots, pumps, sandals, house shoes and loafers)
- A few accessories (pashmina shawl, scarves, belts, hats, gloves)

Undergarments, nightwear, and swimwear are a separate category, but should be chosen as carefully and thoughtfully as the rest. Why keep shapeless old nightshirts you no longer wear, and a six-month supply of tights? Small details like these say a lot about your standards, good sense and femininity.

SHOPPING, BUDGETING AND
CARING FOR YOUR CLOTHES

'The department store encourages the cult of the body,
beauty, flirtation and fashion. Women go there as they go
to church, to pass the time; it is an occupation, a place of
exaltation for womankind, the theatre of the war between
their passion for fine clothes and their husband's budget
and ultimately, the whole drama of existance, above
and beyond the call of beauty.'

Émile Zola, *Au Bonheur des Dames*

Good clothes and careful make-up radiate positive energy. A woman should pay attention, above all, to her health, her beauty and her finances.

Fight passivity. You can change. You can become radiant. Self-confidence is achieved at the expense of a little time spent on personal grooming and self-esteem.

Set a budget for your wardrobe, just as you would for food or your children's education. Dressing well is not a luxury; it is part of a balanced life. Our clothes are our outer envelopes: no one should feel guilty about wanting to look their best. A smart appearance is as important as a decent place to live, or refined tastes. It is part of a greater whole – a question of balance.

Distinguish the things you like and want from the things you really need. Then think about cost.

Expensive clothes are most likely to withstand being worn over a long period of time. The more expensive they are, the more wear you will get out of them.

Choose classic styles, tried and tested labels, clothes that are easy to care for. Well-off people are schooled in the art of investing in expensive classics. Start with a pair of black leather shoes that you can wear with everything.

When you choose a new piece, make sure you can wear it with five other items from your wardrobe. Apply this rule to each new purchase.

Never buy anything simply because 'it's a bargain'.

Organise your wardrobe. Clothes that are folded, hung, aired and protected correctly last longer. Simple as that.

Put seasonal clothes away in another place once you've finished wearing them for the year. Your wardrobe will be less cluttered and confused.

Show your clothes the same respect as your body. Perfume your wardrobes, protect woollens from mites by storing them in sealed bags scented with a small guest soap. Invest in good quality wooden hangers and throw out all the fiddly wire and plastic models you've acquired from the dry cleaners or shopping.

Beautiful coat hangers, all the same (with men's and women's sizes arranged separately), will give your wardrobe the feel of a luxury boutique, making each change of clothes a pleasure. I love the musical knocking of wood on wood!

TRAVEL BAGS

Too many bags, or one very heavy bag, can be a costly waste of time, money and energy (left luggage charges, taxis, long waits at baggage carrousels, sore muscles, irritability). Take one multi-purpose body and hair shampoo (perfect for handwashing your clothes, too), one moisturising oil for hair, nails and body, and nail varnish remover in the form of wipes (they take up far less space than a bag of cotton pads and a bottle, with no danger of leaks).

Three bags are all you need: one travel bag (into which you can pack your clutch for evening outings), one good-sized handbag, and your priceless, essential vanity case.

YOUR VANITY CASE

Using delightful objects – phials, bottles, caskets and pouches – is one of the great pleasures of any beauty ritual. A vanity case should be used every day, not simply when travelling. Chief among a woman's vital possessions, it is her secret garden and loyal servant: a place to keep medicines, beauty products, jewellery and personal items, always ready for an unexpected trip or weekend invitation, safe in the knowledge that your sun cream and eyebrow tweezers haven't been left behind.

Your vanity case is the first thing you open in your hotel room, and your ally for a clean and tidy bathroom at home. Hunting for your toothbrush at the bottom of a suitcase after a fifteen-hour flight is never fun, not forgetting the space all your essentials for personal comfort and grooming can take up in a handbag or suitcase – those little bottles, your hairdryer and curlers, slippers, sewing and nail kits. A good vanity case is the best way to ensure you never own more items than it can hold – but remember to check with your airline what you can take in the cabin in the way of cosmetics and skincare and what must go in the hold.

YOUR HANDBAG, YOUR WORLD

Each day is a journey, and everything you need along the way must be carried in your bag: keys, money, your phone, diary, make-up, medication. Your bag is an extension of you. It spends more time close to you than any item of clothing. Choose it well.

The contents of a woman's bag speak volumes about the things she wants to keep hidden: her chaos or hyper-organisation, her dreams, her mess, her sweet tooth, her sex life, her hygiene obsession, her white lies . . .

Some women hide behind their handbag. It becomes a social status symbol, their secret garden. It should be beautiful (so that you don't need to take a different one out every morning), light-weight (no more than one and a half kilos when full), with well-designed inner pockets (so you don't spend ten minutes searching for a paper tissue or a train ticket), and of the very best quality.

Buying a really good bag is a wise investment. It is better to have one really fine model than ten that will barely last a season, leaving you wondering what to do with them after that.

Have just one bag, but know how to use it elegantly at all times.

Ignore the pressures of consumerism: choose a bag that will serve you and be a source of pleasure for years to come.

Your bag is your intimate companion. It communicates a personality of its own, beyond that of its user. A woman carries the whole world, *her* world, her lifestyle, in her bag. A handbag plays a decorative, protective, and social role. Its psychological repercussions are boundless. It reflects its user's aspirations, occupation and activities, it contains her dreams and secrets. It is a woman's one private space, into which men have never been, and never will be allowed to peek. It is part of her identity. Clearly, a good bag isn't our only ally when it comes to getting the most out of life, but it certainly helps.

In the fifties, women invested serious money in a good bag and pair of matching shoes. The fifties woman had her own model made to order, as a key component of her personal style: ready-to-wear fashion and accessories had yet to be invented. Everything was made to measure, in a woman's own image.

Nowadays, very few women can wear haute couture (a question of shape as much as cost), but no one needs a runway figure to wear a really good bag. An expensive bag can be a great way to offset a more modest outfit. Paired with a simple dress or a plain city suit, a bag can add a splash of colour, and balance a silhouette.

Handbags today come in an infinite variety of styles, but the great classics remain (the Hermès Kelly, the tote . . .), as if their very existence were rooted deep in the female subconscious. Nothing can dislodge them.

Today's woman spends more and more time out of the home, carrying more and more things with her. Be careful to choose a bag with a strong lining (moleskin, for example), fitted with multiple pockets – this will avoid supplementing its weight with extras like make-up bags, spectacle cases or chunky wallets. Any intelligently designed bag will include individual compartments for a compact, a mobile phone, glasses, driving licence, cards, a hook for a key chain, etc.

We may be unable to control the world, but our bag transports us to the centre of our own universe – a place of perfect order, luxury and sensuous delight.

—

CHECKLIST: A FUNCTIONAL,
BEAUTIFUL BAG SHOULD BE

- As attractive inside as out (e.g. the Launer bags carried by Queen Elizabeth II of Great Britain).
- Costly (fine quality) but simply styled (e.g. Jackie Kennedy's Cassini bags).
- Decorative, adding a touch of elegance whether left on a sofa or placed at your feet.
- The perfect fashion accessory, whether worn on the arm or carried at the knee.
- Easy to handle, open and close.
- A source of secret pleasure each time you use it.
- Adaptable but always attractive (in three, seven or ten years' time). In fine leather, with quality metal parts, a good bag will last several decades. A brand-new bag is never beautiful. Be patient . . .
- Neutral, to coordinate with your wardrobe (except your evening clutch, which can function as a piece of jewellery).
- Crafted in soft leather: a fine skin will patinate over time, and indicates the animal was reared in decent conditions, and well fed. (Avoid patent leathers.)
- Showerproof.
- Have a strap neither too short when worn on the shoulder, nor too long when carried on the arm.
- Feature metal studs in the base so that it can be placed on the floor without fear of staining.
- In 'your size', like a coat or a hat, so that it will flatter your

shape. Choose it as part of the 'complete picture' you present to the world (bags that are too small make you look bigger, while oversized models are cumbersome and intrusive).

- Designed without sharp corners (the antidote to femininity and softness), or overly capacious, plump forms (leading to inevitable clutter inside).
- Never more than one and a half kilos in weight when full.
- Filled with pleasing things – telling details that speak volumes about you: a tactile leather diary, a neat wallet, a small, immaculate, white monogrammed handkerchief.

2

In praise of minimalism

Time: waste less, make the most of more

TODAY IS OUR MOST PRECIOUS POSSESSION

'A day of life is more precious than ten thousand pieces of gold ... People who hate death should love life.'

Yoshida Kenkō, *Essays in Idleness* (tr. Donald Keene)

Each new day is the only thing we truly possess. Today is our whole life. Not yesterday, not tomorrow. The present is sacred, the only time we have. If we fail to take advantage of the present moment, we won't do so at some hypothetical point in the future. But 'having time' is not important in itself: the quality of the moment is what matters.

Do not fall into the trap of thinking you must do whatever you want straight away, before it's too late. Whatever you do now will prepare you for the things you will do in future. Everything you do is cumulative.

PEOPLE WANT MORE TIME, THEN 'KILL TIME'

There may be times when you have nothing to do, when you have too much time on your hands. Try to understand exactly what's happening, and to examine and identify your reactions. This is the first step to overcoming issues and moving on.

We often complain that we are wasting time, losing time, short of time. But a person should be able to wait two or three hours for a train, alone, doing nothing, not even with a book, and still not feel bored. Life is far more enjoyable when we cultivate the habit of losing ourselves in our own thoughts: this is a precious gift that brings great happiness. We spend too much time regretting the past, stuck in the present, or worrying about the future. In so doing, we ruin the time we have.

One of the most effective ways to make the most of each moment is to take charge of yourself. Try to do as many things as possible by yourself, for yourself. People often become miserable or depressed because they have nothing to do. Each morning, show your gratitude for the day ahead. What the day brings is unimportant, what matters is what you make of it.

TAKE A BREAK

'It is never too late to do nothing at all.'

Confucius

Go on holiday. Organise long weekends. Get away to a quiet place, 'off grid', far from the hustle and bustle of the world, from your daily cares and concerns. Find a place to stay where meals are included, where you can get away from it all and think.

Collect information about a range of places to suit your different moods and needs. Save them up for those times when you'd love to get away but are too tired to decide where would suit you best.

Take very little with you: too much baggage ruins the simple pleasure of your outing, and the room you will sleep in while you are away. One change of clothes, one toothbrush, a pen and notebook are all you need. Don't burden yourself with material concerns. Most of the time, we are preoccupied and consumed by our material possessions. We need a break from them, too.

Try getting up earlier from time to time. Take breakfast in a pleasant café, or prepare a picnic to enjoy later, at sunset.

'Changing gear' from time to time helps you to avoid becoming bogged down in routine, to live each moment with the intensity it deserves.

By simplifying our lives, we find new reserves of energy. We are better able to deal with people and situations. With minimal possessions, the present moment assumes greater intensity. We appreciate the things around us: there is less to do, more time to think, dream or just laze. Learn how to spend an entire day at home reading poetry, cooking, burning incense, drinking a glass of fine wine, watching the moon. Simplify your domestic tasks and find time to develop your creativity, pamper your body and sharpen your mental faculties.

THE JOYS OF IDLENESS

'I drink my tea, I eat my rice. I spend time as the moments present themselves, contemplating the stream that flows below, and looking up at the mountains. Such freedom! Such peace!'

A Taoist

Idleness should be a sought-after luxury, not a form of inertia. It should be savoured, appreciated, accepted as a heaven-sent gift, a 'stolen' moment.

With few possessions and a little organisation, idleness becomes a privilege. There are too many things demanding our care and attention. Instead of devoting time to objects, we should make ourselves available for other things.

Too many people are driven by passions that are, in reality, a form of passivity. They are running away from themselves. In fact, taking time to stop, sit and contemplate our experiences and identity is the highest form of activity. But this is only possible once we have achieved inner freedom and independence.

SHARPEN YOUR SENSES FOR LIFE

Learning to live mindfully is the basis of all Buddhist, Taoist and yogic teaching, and the belief systems of America's Navajo First Nation. The same philosophy underpins the writings of numerous artists and thinkers, including Emerson, Thoreau and Whitman.

Mindfulness opens the doors to immense reserves of creativity, intelligence, determination and wisdom. Living mindfully means keeping your spirit open and free.

Zen philosophy requires us to give the smallest tasks our full and complete attention. We should strive for complete focus in everything we do, whether reading, listening to music or contemplating a landscape. When we live in and for the present, we do not experience tiredness. Most of the time, people are more exhausted by the thought of all they have to do, than by what they have actually done. This is why indolent people are often depressed. Research has proved that inactivity slows the metabolism and leads to a drop in blood pressure.

Since we must get on with life, it behoves us to do so with good grace, and to accomplish our tasks without question.

REPETITIVE, EVERYDAY TASKS: AN EXERCISE IN CONCENTRATION

We should not fear the future. We should fear the many moments we let slip here and now. The answer is simple: develop our ability to focus, and reject non-essential, 'parasitical' thoughts. The only thing that matters is what you are doing now, in the present. Take things slowly, and focus on the moment. The ability to influence the quality of the moment in hand is one of our most precious gifts. Just as each of our cells contains the genes of all the rest, so each moment is a reflection of every other moment in our lives.

PREPARE FOR THE UNEXPECTED

In Zen temples, the monks and nuns gather each evening to discuss what food will be prepared and eaten the next day. Thinking ahead is vital, even while focusing on the present.

A state of preparedness for all eventualities brings enhanced serenity: an unexpected visit from a friend, an emergency, a last-minute invitation! This state of preparedness is the best way to live fully in the present.

Someone told me the story of a Japanese woman suffering from a condition that meant she might be hospitalised at any moment. For twenty years she spent each evening preparing for her possible absence from home the next day – she would only go to bed once the meals were prepared, clothes ironed and put away, housework finished and her small bag packed and ready in the hallway. More than anything, she wanted to be sure her absence would not inconvenience her family: it was her way of accepting her condition with as much grace and serenity as possible.

SANCTIFY THE SIMPLEST ACTIONS:
ENRICH YOUR LIFE WITH RITUALS

"'What's a ritual?" said the little prince.
"Something else that is too readily forgotten," said the fox.
"It is what makes one day different from another,
or one hour from the other hours.'"

Antoine de Saint-Exupéry tr. Ros and Chloe Schwartz

Simple actions like eating, conversing or cleaning the home can be sanctified as rituals.

Ritualise your first sip of coffee each morning, your make-up routine, an afternoon's window shopping, the purchase of a long-desired object, the wait for a loved one's footsteps on the stairs, day-dreaming on a rainy Sunday, a night watching DVDs with a bowl of seeded pomegranates, a Monday morning full of new resolutions.

Imagine yourself living like Grace Kelly, in a film where everything occurs naturally and easily – the kind of person for whom the world stands still when, nonchalantly, she takes a filmy negligee from her overnight case.

What are your personal rituals? What do they bring to your life?

Montaigne said that a life lived to the full is a life enriched and nourished by ritual. Rituals bring comfort when we stumble under the pressures and demands of everyday existence.

Living is above all a question of awareness. You are the only person who can improve your environment and personalise the details that accompany your rituals.

Knowing how to live well is a cultivated habit, and rituals can help. Once we recognise their significance and charm, they can enrich other areas, too, bringing satisfaction, mystery, peace and order. Rituals sanctify everyday life and open up new dimensions in our world.

Don't feel guilty if you fail to keep to certain rituals: this means they do not contribute as much to your happiness as you thought they did.

A ritual should be a source of extreme satisfaction. If so, respect it and practice it zealously and with as much enthusiasm as possible.

SOME SUGGESTED RITUALS

THE WRITING RITUAL

'I have my rituals, a meticulous scenario: my pens, a special type of paper, a precise time of day, the things around me strictly arranged, my coffee at the right temperature ... '

Dominique Rolin

The act of writing may be enhanced by careful arrangement of the things around you, the paper and ink best adapted to the task, the presentation and format of your notes, the comfort of the chair you sit in, the penumbra around your brightly lit desk.

THE BATH RITUAL

Choose minimal products of the finest quality for your face, hair and bath. Place everything to hand before you get into the water: music, candles, a glass of sparkling water, the clothes you'll wear next, even jewellery. Leave the bathroom spotless, for a totally cleansed feeling.

THE SHOPPING RITUAL

Cultivate your inner hunter-gatherer when shopping: seek only the best. Fresh, quality foodstuffs are essential for your enjoyment and health. Shopping is an activity that requires imagination, good sense and enthusiasm. Take a strong, sizeable basket, a wallet set aside for household expenses only, and your list. Remember, sourcing the finest, untreated produce, tasty fruit, really good bread, and well-run, privately owned stores takes time and perseverance.

THE FLOWER RITUAL

The power of flowers . . . Once a week, treat yourself to a bunch of flowers. They will brighten your home and your mood, even if you choose a single rose for your bedside table, or chrysanthemums for the bathroom. Flowers add a fresh touch. They are also said to lower adrenaline levels at times of stress. Like fruit and fresh air, they are indispensable to our well-being.

A TIME FOR EVERYTHING

Walk for half an hour every day.

Take a nap when you can, even five minutes at your desk.

Look at an album of your favourite photographs. Your whole life is here. It will show you the moments, people and places that have made you what you are, loved you, changed you. Looking at these pictures, you will rediscover yourself.

Devote fifteen minutes of your day to a project that is important to you (reading, planning a trip, making a family tree . . .).

Only ever do one thing at a time.

—

Learn to say no gracefully and firmly.

Live life at a slower pace, working less. Refuse to take on extra hours, or work part time if you are able.

Avoid routine. If you drink coffee, try tea. Vary your journey to work.

Own little.

Schedule your housework.

Buy all of your shopping in one session, once a week.

Keep your desktop free of paperwork, except for immediate, ongoing tasks. A permanent pile of documents is a constant reminder of what remains to be done. It's a source of stress, and will blur your focus.

Answer emails and letters quickly, and never leave a task half-done.

Money: your servant, not your master

MONEY IS ENERGY

'A creative economy is the fuel of magnificence.'

Ralph Waldo Emerson

We complicate our lives when we fail to give money its proper importance. We should strive to understand its influence on each aspect of our lives. Think about the relationship between money and nature, ideas, pleasure, self-respect, the habitat, the environment, friends, society... Money is implicated in all of these.

Money is a force: a force that structures our lives, whether we want it to or not. Healthy circulation is a sign of a healthy body. When money circulates freely in our lives, we are in good financial health.

Obviously, this is more difficult if we are on a low income, and forced to count every penny. But are we making efficient use of the money we have? To take one example: buying only fresh vegetables, and small amounts of meat or fish instead of industrially produced ready meals will be as satisfying to the palate as it is to the bank balance.

Money is a resource that we allow to slip through our fingers: our uncontrolled impulses prevent us from taking a cool, clear look at things.

Only you can know what money means to you. Money is energy in reserve. Being satisfied with little is one of the best ways to retain that energy. If we spend our money on things that are of no value to us, our energy reserves are depleted.

MAKE MONEY YOUR SLAVE

*'When money is plentiful, it's a man's world. When it is
scarce, it's a woman's world. The woman's instinct comes
into play when all else has failed. She is the one who
will find work. And this is why the world keeps turning,
in spite of everything.'*

Article from a women's magazine, October 1932

Have you ever tried working out how much money has passed
through your hands since the day you received your first penny
under the pillow from the tooth fairy? How much money do you have
today?

We waste too much on useless items and short-term treats.
Big-ticket investments are not a drain on our financial resources,
but the thousands of small items we've bought, and then forgotten
all about, are. Leaving a restaurant tired, having eaten too much, and
with an indigestible bill in inverse proportion to your enjoyment of
the meal is the ultimate definition of waste. Waste means thinking
you've got a bargain, then regretting your purchase. It means buying
a cheap sweater that loses its colour or shrinks the first time it's
washed, or a poor-quality mattress that hurts your back.

Economising, and spending within your means, on the other
hand, is a positive choice: it delivers security. Everyone should
devise their own 'security-serenity-savings' plan. Reducing your
needs to the strict minimum is the surest way to achieve it.

Divide your money into two parts: the first part is assigned to
maintaining your frugal lifestyle, the second – what's left, if any – is
for whims and fancies. Save in order to work less, not buy more.

With savings behind us, we feel positive and happier, because we are less anxious about the future.

Make money your slave, not your master. Never be financially dependent on others, and never enter the vicious circle of borrowing and debt. Never spend more than you earn, and save a little each month. This seems simple enough, but if so, why are so many people in debt, living beyond their means, and bitter as a result?

THE PRICE OF DISORDER

The price of disorder is a life overburdened with things we wouldn't miss if they weren't there: the things we had forgotten all about until we found them at the bottom of the cupboard, in a trunk in the attic. Things that are there in plain sight all the time: they stand alongside things we use every day, but they get in the way.

Many items are not worth keeping. We pay insurance on homes full of superfluous items, and spend time scrubbing paint and rust and dust off old objects, to 'bring them back to life' – a waste of time and energy. There are so many more enriching ways to live your life: travel, learning a new skill, sport, walking, cooking or simply resting and contemplating a beautiful landscape.

Disorder means we often end up owning the same thing twice, cluttering our space for no reason.

Education and morality have sunk so low in today's society that materialism and acquisitiveness are actively, cynically and hypo-critically, encouraged. We are blinded and enslaved by fashion (in clothes, leisure, food . . .). Few people understand the true value of money, or treat it with proper seriousness. Money lubricates the machinery of life. One of the great Zen ideals is for an individual to be able to wear all their possessions (a change of clothes, a bowl, a pair of chopsticks, a razor and a nail-trimmer) around their neck, in a box. The modesty and simplicity of his accoutrements is the Buddhist monk's tacit challenge to the modern world. Striving for minimalism in this way is a positive response to the deep dissatisfaction engendered by today's consumer society.

ECONOMISE: EXERCISE RESTRAINT, AND ASSESS YOUR TRUE NEEDS

The one thing we all try to hold on to for as long as possible is our health. We can all achieve better health by eating better quality food, and less of it, by respecting the tenets of preventative medicine, by positive thinking, and by taking ourselves in hand.

We should apply the same principles to our possessions: our household appliances, clothes and objects. We live with so much excess that we find it hard to contemplate the alternative. Never having known hunger or want, we believe our present abundance will never end.

KEEP SIMPLE ACCOUNTS, TAKE CONTROL OF YOUR LIFE

Keep track of all your earnings and expenses. This will help you to economise more, manage your finances better, and simplify your life. Most of our money-management problems stem from thoughtless spending habits rather than uncontrolled impulses and sprees. Try, for example, to calculate what you spend on food treats, and diet products in an effort to lose the weight gained; not to mention on dental bills, make-up and cleansing products to correct your dull complexion.

Try to make a point of knowing exactly how much money you have and what you can spend. You'll find it easier to put off buying that coat you've been eyeing, but which you can't afford right now. Make a note of all expenses: this will help you to avoid frittering your hard-earned money away with thoughtless spending.

When the American philosopher Henry David Thoreau lived in isolation for two years, in Walden, he was delighted to be able to count his financial operations on the fingers of one hand.

Have only one bank account and one or two credit cards.

Twice a month, set aside some quiet time at your kitchen table, with a good cup of coffee and some music, to do your accounts. Ritualise the payment of bills with serenity, not as a painful chore. Know that you are in control of your finances.

Apart from big-ticket items – an apartment or a house – avoid borrowing as far as possible. Avoid impulse buys at all times. Your credit card should be kept for emergencies only: as soon as you use it, you are spending more than the cost price. Bank loans are a form of commerce, too.

3

Ethics and aesthetics

Beauty is a need

MINIMALISM AND BEAUTY
(THE TEA CEREMONY)

'The Philosophy of Tea is not mere aestheticism in the ordinary acceptance of the term, for it expresses conjointly with ethics and religion our whole point of view about man and nature. It is hygiene, for it enforces cleanliness; it is economics, for it shows comfort in simplicity rather than in the complex and costly; it is moral geometry, inasmuch as it defines our sense of proportion to the universe.'

Kazuko Okakura, *The Book of Tea*

Oriental aesthetics are rooted in Taoism, but Zen makes them applicable to everyday life. Kazuko Okakura's *Book of Tea* aims to make its readers 'votaries' of the philosophy of tea, and 'aristocrats of taste'.

The tea ceremony is a ritual incorporating both aesthetic and philosophical values, as an expression of discipline and social relationships. The spiritual 'tea' it dispenses is a pared-down, simplified, tightly packaged set of strict rules highlighting principles of purity and serenity. The tea ceremony scales great heights. It is a pinnacle of learning about material things, and the things of the spirit. Mind and matter become one, and enhanced beauty is the result.

Artistry is fundamental to everything: it is present in gestures, objects, clothing, our personal conduct. Many people collect objects, but few cultivate the spirit. With few possessions, we develop a closer attachment to the objects that can help us to achieve purification. The values underpinning the practice of the tea ceremony are those of our daily life.

The tea is prepared with the minimum of utensils and gestures, according to strict rules. Once the rules have been learned and applied, it becomes possible to transcend form and attain the highest spheres of consciousness.

The tea ceremony is a living example of minimalism as an ethical concept: it is a quest for beauty, and a protracted examination of how a result may be attained with as much grace and economy as possible. For the Japanese, the appreciation of beauty is a sacred, almost devotional activity, exemplified in the practice of the Buddhist monk or nun, seated in the lotus position, motionless while the incense stick continues to burn, surrounded by gilded statues and candles, elevating the spirit to a world of serenity and beauty. The monk lives a spartan life, paradoxically surrounded by elaborate, carved and lacquered woodwork.

The minimalism and beauty of places like the Zen garden in Kyoto, the Ryoanji Temple or the stunning temple sanctuaries of Korea (still relatively little known to tourists) bring us face to face with the infinite in our own being.

THE AESTHETIC CONCEPT OF WABI-SABI

'Not a colour to disturb the tone of the room, not a sound to mar the rhythm of things, not a gesture to obtrude on the harmony, not a word to break the unity of the surroundings, all movements to be performed simply and naturally – such were the aims of the tea ceremony ... Everything is sober in tint from the ceiling to the floor; the guests themselves have carefully chosen garments of unobtrusive colours. The mellowness of age is over all, everything suggestive of recent acquirement being tabooed save only the one note of contrast furnished by the bamboo dipper and the linen napkin, both immaculately white and new.'

Kazuko Okakura, *The Book of Tea*

Wabi-sabi is rooted in a system of positive aesthetic values experienced through the choices of an individual who has spent a period of time isolated from the world, and is therefore better able to appreciate the small details of each aspect of everyday life. It conceptualises the fact that what the universe destroys, it also builds. It celebrates the humble, hidden beauty of incomplete and imperfect things.

Material things esteemed by connoisseurs of *wabi-sabi* point the way to an ultimate, transcendental state: rice paper for soft, filtered light, the crackled surface of dried mud, rust and tarnish on metal, the knotted roots of trees, straw, rocks covered in lichen . . .

The Japanese concept of *wabi-sabi* was established in the fourteenth century CE as a pure, idealised, extreme form of minimalism.

As with homeopathy, the essence of *wabi-sabi* is dispensed in infinitesimally small doses: the smaller the dose, the more profound its impact.

In Shintoism, the emphasis on frugality as a way of life has contributed much to the practical application of a system of aesthetic values focused on using the humblest, simplest spaces and materials as efficiently and effectively as possible.

Random, naturally occurring irregularities are considered the height of taste: knotted wood, accidental motifs produced when firing pottery, the shape of an eroded rock.

Zen philosophy is wary of art objects and the signed imprint of an artist on a work. It requires a man to be neither master nor slave of things and others, nor a slave to himself and his emotions, principles or desires. In Zen, beauty is a state of non-preoccupation, of liberation from all things. Once this state has been achieved, everything becomes beautiful. It is a state of mind, the acceptance of the inevitable, the appreciation of the cosmic order, material poverty and spiritual wealth.

BEAUTY IS A NEED

'If from all your wealth,
Two meagre loaves remain,
Sell one, and with your gains,
Buy hyacinths to feed your soul.'

Muslih-uddin Sa'di (thirteenth-century Persian poet)

Japanese people have always embraced minimalism – but a form of minimalism of which beauty is an intrinsic part. A century ago, even the humblest dwellings were models of cleanliness, and everyone knew the art of writing poetry, arranging flowers and serving meals with delicacy and absolute refinement. Zen is not merely a religion: it is above all an ethical system. As such, it serves as a model for anyone choosing to embrace a minimalist lifestyle. We all have a profound need for order, and Zen liberates us from confusion in all its forms, even material or physical disorder. Zen teaches us that the simpler we are, the stronger we become.

The sound of music, the texture of a soft fabric, the fragrance of a rose: we are naturally drawn to these things. They are sources of energy and pleasure.

Beauty in all its forms is indispensable to our well-being. As human beings, we need more beauty than we realise, or may seem reasonable. Our soul needs beauty just as our body needs air, water and food. Without beauty, we become sad, depressed, sometimes even deranged. Beauty is an invitation to contemplation. It absorbs us completely. Shakespeare, Bach, Ozu – all connect us directly to life itself.

Aesthetics and ethics are linked. The Japanese embrace beauty as a way of preserving their love of life. True luxury is defined as a condition we feel naturally comfortable with, almost without noticing: a good-quality armchair with the aroma of fine leather, a cashmere throw, crystal water glasses, a white linen tablecloth, plain white porcelain plates that retain the heat, thick Egyptian cotton napkins, a room devoid of knick-knacks, with a wood fire for the winter months, a discreet bouquet of flowers, seasonal vegetables from a nearby garden.

False luxury is whatever is 'bought ostentatiously', perhaps with the aim of reproducing a fashionable interior from the pages of a magazine: hi-tech furniture devoid of comfort, food prepared using imaginative but often indigestible ingredients, holidays spent in 'trending', overcrowded hotspots, so that we need tranquillisers to recover.

LIVING ELEGANTLY, TO PERFECTION

'In secret he practised austerities which no one even suspected. But his long apprenticeship to stoic duty had not hardened him into self-righteousness. ... In everything, his taste was exquisite, whether for people, objects, manners ...'

Marguerite Yourcenar, *Memoirs of Hadrian,*
tr. by Grace Frick

Doing everything with style brings an infinitely richer life. Style means brushing your hair before breakfast, playing soft music at mealtimes, avoiding plastic and synthetic material wherever possible in your everyday surroundings. It means using your silverware every day, and not only when you have guests.

In the United States, during the Great Depression of the 1930s, money was far less important than style. Almost every family had lost out, so that money was no longer a distinguishing factor from one household to the next. What counted instead were vocabulary and diction, education, moral values and a taste for things of quality. Everyone used their finest things every day, and put flowers on the table at mealtimes. We can always strive for greater perfection in life. Details are enormously important. When everything is just right, we feel in balance. Perfect details leave us free to concentrate on 'bigger' things. But when small details are neglected, they are a source of constant irritation.

Style and beauty help us to progress, and surpass ourselves. In Japan, beautiful deportment and gestures express the perfect balance between intent and effort. The right way to handle chopsticks, or the perfect posture when sitting on a tatami mat, all are connected to an attitude of asceticism practised with grace and rigour.

'Less for more' order and cleanliness

THE ETHICS OF CLEANLINESS

*'Shining cleanliness, the perfect order ... that spotless and
sweet-smelling kitchen ... All the tranquillity of my life
depends upon [the housekeeper's work, which is] in itself a
satisfaction, a pride.'*

George Gissing, *The Private Papers of Henry Ryecroft*

Originally, the tea ceremony was a series of simple but austere practices aimed at developing a sense of discipline and precision, a means of 'setting the spirit in order'. We have only to look at the face of a ninety-year-old Buddhist monk or nun to see the lifelong benefits of its practice.

Buddhist monks or nuns accomplish housework, cleaning and gardening as contemplative exercises in their own right. They respect and care for their surroundings, because they know this world has given them life. For them, the broom is a sacred object. When a Buddhist monk sweeps the floor, first and foremost he is sweeping his soul.

Zen teaching shows how we can purify ourselves through housework and cleaning. Returning an object to its proper place, tidying a room, and closing the door on a spotless and ordered space symbolise our ability to set the world to rights. Cleaning sweeps away non-essential accretions to reveal the essence of mankind and nature.

Each tiny patch of cleanliness brings instant comfort. A household god lurks behind your saucepans – make them shine like a new penny! Everyday tasks are an important part of life. Each day, each new season may be the best yet.

In Japan, housework is not seen as degrading. Children at school, workers in offices, retired people out in the streets . . . everyone starts their day by doing a small share of cleaning. Taxpayers' money is not wasted on street cleaners or toilet attendants. Housework is an essential part of life. Cleaning, sweeping, washing and cooking keep people fit and encourage them to take ownership of their lives and surroundings. A person who keeps active providing for his daily needs will not suffer stroke, or experience torpor, or mental apathy, when ideas drift and float like clouds.

Every right-thinking man or woman should be capable of cleaning up after themselves, even if they have the means to pay someone else. Do not neglect the material world: it is a source of beauty and goodness, too. Cleaning your own house is like brushing your own teeth: a vital need.

Embellish everything you touch, even when performing the most basic tasks. Even menial actions can be performed with aesthetic sensitivity. Every action, even the simplest aspect of everyday existence, can be accomplished with dignity as a creative exercise in its own right.

Three helpful maxims:
A place for everything, and everything in its place.
Tidiness saves time and frees the memory.
Good work begins with clean and tidy surroundings.

FRUGALITY, CLEANLINESS AND TIDINESS

'Order is the shape upon which beauty depends.'

Pearl Buck

Folding your sheets into neat piles is a form of defence in a chaotic world. We are powerless in the face of disease, death and nightmares, but our tidy cupboards stand as proof that can we can and do control our own tiny corner of the universe.

Give yourself the small satisfaction of folding and tidying your laundry, then. Clean the washbasin after you've used it. Close the top of your cereal packet neatly and firmly, and put it back in its proper place. Savour each act: it delivers a small pulse of pleasure and contentment, even beauty. Appreciate and cultivate secret delights such as these.

Beauty alone makes life worth living. Creating a beautiful life is the highest vocation. Remember: beauty is present in small details, in order and cleanliness, in things that support and nourish us.

When we create an ordered environment, we order our inner selves, too. Every drawer full of clutter emptied, every cupboard tidied, every productive effort of organisation and simplification reaffirms our sense of control over our own lives.

THE ART OF HOUSEWORK

Make housework a moment of real pleasure. Wear appropriate clothes, put on some music, and prepare for a workout! Try not to use too many different products: these can be a source of clutter in themselves. Keep to just two or three quality products (bleach is still and always will be the most effective) and keep them in an accessible place. If you live in a house with several storeys, keep a set of cleaning products on each floor: this will minimise tiring legwork.

Keep a proper cleaning cupboard for your broom, vacuum cleaner, buckets – the objects we all love to hate.

HOUSEHOLD TIPS

- Nail a grill tray to the inside of a kitchen cupboard door: perfect for holding knives, ladles, etc.
- Stand trays and chopping boards on your worktop between bookends.
- Fold bath towels in three lengthways, so that no stitched edges are left showing.
- Keep cotton wool balls, brushes and other beauty accessories in transparent glass jars.
- Wrap electric cords and lengths of string in figures of eight around your thumb and ring finger before putting them away.
- Use a large bin bag as an overall for heavy-duty work.
- Install rails and hooks in your hall for bags, coats, gloves, scarves.
- Keep a stack of baskets ready for clean linens, sorted after washing, per category and per room.
- Label and name folders containing documents.
- Do not cover food with cling film, as after a while it becomes sticky and unpleasant.

- Stick memos on the inside of your cupboard doors.
- Use a fork in a glass as a cardholder.
- Keep photographic negatives in empty Kleenex boxes.
- Keep each complete set of bedlinen inside one of its pillowcases.
- Keep empty bags in order of size (small, medium, large) in three empty tissue boxes.
- Keep tins on their sides in a drawer, so you can read the labels easily.
- Take inspiration from storage solutions in shops (pigeonholing).
- Cut out circles of industrial felt or other thick fabric and insert them between your best plates.
- Keep plenty of small hand towels and tea towels nearby when cooking.
- Use a grease-busting microfibre cloth or a traditional brush for washing up.
- Soak your small kitchen sponges in a bowl of water with a little bleach overnight.
- Store fresh vegetables in Tupperware containers lined with damp kitchen paper.
- Clean your ceiling with a small towel fixed to a broom with an elastic band.
- Reduce electrostatic dust (around your TV or computer) by wiping with a very slightly damp cloth and a drop of conditioning shampoo.
- Degrease your kitchen extractor fan by soaking it in water and a drop of washing-up liquid overnight.

- Avoid houseplants with small leaves (they drop more, and are more difficult to dust).
- Make I–2cm incisions in a cleaning sponge, to make it easier to wipe along awkward places (sliding door rails, hanging rails, slatted blinds).
- Remove bobbles from woollen sweaters using a Scotch-Brite or other abrasive sponge.
- Use a small fitment or hand-held cleaner to vacuum the inside of your fridge.
- Place a cotton wool ball soaked in essential oils in the filter of your vacuum cleaner.
- Never use too much detergent in your laundry (it will spoil your clothes, but line the pockets of the manufacturers).
- Use a net bag for washing sweaters and delicate items.

KEEP IT SIMPLE

1. Never accept anything you don't want.
2. Don't feel guilty about throwing or giving things away.
3. Don't accumulate perfume samples in your bathroom.
4. Imagine your house has burned to the ground and make a list of what you would really need to buy.
5. Followed by a list of what you wouldn't need to buy.
6. Photograph objects you love but never use, then get rid of them.
7. Think about your needs in light of your experience. When in doubt, throw it out.

—

8. Get rid of anything you haven't used at least once in the past year.

9. Adopt a personal mantra: *I want only essential things*.

10. Understand that less brings more.

11. Know the difference between your needs and your desires.

12. See how long you can cope without an object you thought was indispensable.

13. Eliminate as many material things as possible.

14. Tidying and reorganising involves more than simply moving things around.

15. Remember, simplification doesn't mean getting rid of things you love, but of things that don't contribute to your happiness.

16. Know that nothing is irreplaceable.

17. Decide on the exact numbers of things you want to keep (spoons, sheets, pairs of shoes, etc).

18. Designate a place for each and every thing.

19. Don't accumulate empty boxes, bags or jars.

20. Don't keep more than two outfits for cleaning and chores.

21. Set aside a cupboard for important documents, stationery, spare batteries, receipts, road maps – items that are so often homeless in the home. Inspect each room: one less object is one less thing to dust.

22. Ask yourself: why do I keep that?

23. Imagine your home is 'visited' by thieves. Don't own anything too valuable for them to take.

24. Don't be a prisoner of things bought in error long ago. Repair the wrong by getting rid of them.

25. Try making a list of everything you own. Impossible?

26. And a list of everything you've offloaded already. Any regrets?

27. Remind yourself that offloading whatever irritates you, even sentimental objects, will be good for your well-being.

28. Don't hesitate to swap good for better. You'll experience increased satisfaction.

29. Never settle for second best. The closer everything around you comes to perfection, the greater your serenity.

30. Only buy things when you have money to spare.

31. Change is what keeps a home alive.

32. Trust classic objects that have proved their quality.

33. Organise yourself so that you no longer need to organise yourself: reduce to the max!

34. Reduce the number of activities you're involved in.

35. Ensure that each new object you buy is smaller, by weight and volume.

36. Reject unnecessary gadgetry.

PART II

BODY

'A jade vase is made by repeated polishing.'

Dōgen

Taking care of your body means setting it free. Many women spend time, energy and money creating a beautiful home, cooking for their family and friends, taking care of others, or going out, while ignoring their own body and making excuses – they 'don't have time' for walking, cleansing rituals or a planned diet. What they fail to realise is that, just as the harmony and nobility of a face reflects the intelligence behind it, so the body does, too. But caring for your body and your appearance, taking massages and keeping your joints supple remain low on many Westerners' list of priorities (especially older people). This is a legacy of Judeo-Christian thinking, in which the cult of body is taboo, even sinful. It's worth remembering that public spas, the practice of massage, and teaching on dietetics were widespread in Europe in the Hellenistic and Roman periods, but disappeared with the advent of Christianity. For centuries, Western culture has frowned on the cult of sensible self-care, elegance, the maintenance of a clear complexion, a healthy body and a supple frame. We have neglected our 'physical intelligence' and become lazy, complacent, even dishonest with ourselves and others. In the West, we accept universal healthcare, leisure and abundant food as our right; but do they entitle us to indulge ourselves and lead unhealthy, unbalanced lives, when millions of people around the world lack access to medical treatment or even adequate food?

Why do we accept extra kilos, cholesterol, a dull or blemished complexion, stiff joints and endless visits to the doctor as an inevitable consequence of ageing, while doing nothing to alter our lifestyle, habits and diet?

Living with a body that makes our every movement awkward or uncomfortable is tiring, and robs us of our dignity and independence. We become our own willing slaves!

Our bodies have clearly defined needs. If we overstep those boundaries, it becomes more and more difficult to contain our cravings. Don't neglect your body – your own life, and the lives of others, depend on it. While a wholly self-centred, sybaritic existence filled with nothing but physical activity, food and spa treatments is clearly neglectful of the intellect, we must care for our bodies if we are to live well. And so we must learn (or rediscover) moderation, and the right approach to keeping ourselves supple, cleansed, clean, and disciplined.

The body should not burden the mind and spirit. It should be made ready to support and reflect intellectual activity and the things of the spirit.

1

Your beauty

Finding your own image

BE YOURSELF

'Until one has made himself beautiful he has no right to
approach beauty.'

Kakuzo Okakura

Being beautiful means first and foremost being yourself. Our personal failings and mishaps are opportunities to know ourselves better, and to grow as a result. Beauty is the convergence of a number of factors: self-assurance, pride, presence, allure, vivacity.

A woman is attractive because she feels attractive – hence the importance of self-knowledge and acceptance.

Clothes, make-up, tastes and trends: strive to look like the person you know you truly are. Adopt a pioneering spirit, pushing back the accepted frontiers, especially of age: it's up to us. Many people now live beyond a hundred. Don't accept that old age and ill health inevitably go hand in hand: you can grow older and still become stronger, more energetic, more beautiful. Women who feel tired all the time invariably blame their age, when it is far more likely to be due to the unbalanced functioning of hormones and glands they didn't know existed. They may suffer insomnia, hypoglycaemia, nervous depression, or memory loss; they may find themselves unable to control their cravings for sugary foods. Doctors tell them these glands 'neutralise' emotional shocks, and they can help regain their energy with positive thoughts. Feeling happy in ourselves, and surrounding ourselves with happy people are essential for health and beauty. Laugh, watch a comedy on TV or at the cinema, tell funny stories.

You can decide to change, too: dress differently, swap your morning coffee for a different drink, take another route to work, add a touch of imaginative zest where you feel it is lacking.

Walk, cook, live your personal 'energy'. Enjoyment of life is essential for beauty. Beware of stress, anxiety, anger, sadness and fear: these are your enemies. Practise letting go of negative emotions as lightly and easily as possible: they cannot touch you. This is the best way to preserve your vital resources, and far more effective than a luxury body cream. Try to remain neutral, quietly detached and uninvolved: you will feel more serene, and look more beautiful. Look at yourself in a mirror and identify the tiniest signs of negativity, anxiety, fatigue or anger. Then relax and smile at yourself.

SUPERFICIAL CHARM VERSUS INNER BEAUTY

'But, if you have nothing at all to create, then perhaps
you create yourself.'

Carl Jung, Foreword to Suzuki's *Introduction to Zen Buddhism*

No one can take better care of your body than you can yourself – not your doctor, your beautician, or your make-up adviser. We are responsible for our own bodies and at fault if we neglect them. Why risk losing your figure, ageing prematurely, falling ill? Our health is our most precious possession. We need to realise that we each possess our own special beauty. Why wait to fall ill, and regret that we did nothing to preserve and care for nature's gift?

But physical beauty is only truly radiant when it reflects inner beauty. In Vietnam's Ho Chi Minh City, a quarter of the population don't have a liveable home, yet in the early morning the parks are full of activity. Hundreds of people of all ages are jogging, stretching, warming up; under a nearby tree, a lively group of older ladies stands waiting – they have invested their meagre savings in a set of scales, available to all for a small fee. Everyone engages in sport, everyone watches their weight, everyone wants to take care of their body, their only real 'home.'

Each of us is a gem: we must be polished for our true brilliance to shine forth. Striving to be beautiful and keep fit is as important as creating a work of art: we don't need a canvas and brushes to express ourselves: our bodies and minds are enough. Ageing is a key test of our inner beauty. It grows and manifests itself more and more over time. Genuinely beautiful people are delightful to look at, whatever their age. Style comes with good sense and taste. Style is not limited to your clothes, or your physique; it's an outer sign of inner intelligence. Style is a choice, a concept of self, of what we want to become, and how to get there.

DON'T BE A VICTIM OF YOUR OWN BODY

'A woman should paint her nails until she's ninety.'

Anaïs Nin

If you fail to take care of your body, you will fall victim to its short-comings. Your body is your home. Do not neglect it while you give care to others. Giving comes naturally, with loving – only when we love are we able to give. Commit to loving and caring for your body: you owe it to yourself, your family and everyone else in your life. No one likes to see a neglected home. The same is true of your body.

We have a duty to maintain a clean, well-groomed appearance. No one needs to be 'born beautiful', we can all make ourselves more attractive by keeping to a few simple rules, cultivating self-awareness and making a conscious choice not to abuse our bodies.

As Shakespeare's Ophelia says, 'We know what we are now, but not what we may become.' The desire to be physically pleasing is not superficial – it's a question of respect. Beauty is not always heaven-sent. It's a discipline, and mankind has pursued it since the dawn of time. Physical beauty depends largely on health and self-confidence. By cultivating our inner energy and vitality, we become more active, respond better to the people around us, and feel a greater sense of self-respect.

ASSERT YOUR PRESENCE

'My grandmother kept more signs of her femininity than my
mother. Although her jackets – still in the traditional style –
all became the colour of pale grey, she took particular care
of her long, thick black hair [which she tied up] in a neat bun
at the back of her head, but she always had flowers there ...
She never used shampoo from the shops, but would boil the
fruit of the Chinese honey locust and use the liquid from that ...
She added a final touch by putting on a little water
of osmanthus flowers which she made herself ... She would
paint her eyebrows lightly with a black charcoal pencil and
dab a little powder on her nose ... People noticed her.
She walked proudly, her figure erect, with a restrained
self-consciousness.'

Jung Chang, *Wild Swans: Three Daughters of China*

A person with presence will always make a strong impression. They don't need a perfect figure to be beautiful. The quality of that presence is what we call their 'allure'.

Try to steer your thoughts away from the mediocrities of everyday life. You can find renewal each day, in the choices you make. Refining the attitudes and actions that best reflect your personality is the best way to make your mark, whether lighting incense sticks, composing a bouquet of flowers, brewing tea, or preparing a meal. Find your own way to be comfortable in your skin, and in your mind.

Assert your presence through your personal conduct.

Find the seated posture that suits you best: your pride and

self-esteem will grow. In the Navajo language, anyone who walks with dignity and confidence is said to be 'carrying their beauty'.

AIM FOR TRANSPARENCY

Transparency is the absence of rigidity; it is the quality that allows a person to radiate their inner self. But it can only be achieved through self-fulfilment, confidence and a natural manner, by being responsive and able to overcome any situation, by maintaining your poise and waiting quietly for things yet to come. Unselfconscious, 'automatic' actions and attitudes liberate the mind to concentrate on the simple act of being, with no need to pause and think about the best way to perform a task, or the choices before you. If you are unsure how to accomplish a task, you will spend time mulling over the question before you start. But if you have learned how to proceed, your actions will be automatic. The same principle applies to the arts, languages, domestic chores.

When a person feels good in their own skin, they will feel good everywhere they go.

THINK ABOUT YOUR EXPRESSIONS
AND 'TICKS'

Our physiognomy can show us to our best advantage, or let us down completely. Beauty is a combination of genetics, diet and optimism. It's vital to become aware of your facial expressions: a tense expression reveals your inner stress and maintains it, too. Release the tension from your face, and it will vanish inside, too.

Smile at the world! You'll make yourself happy, and the world will smile back.

PERFECT YOUR ACTIONS

'We are what we repeatedly do. Excellence, then, is not an act, but a habit.'

Aristotle

We reveal ourselves to others through our actions. Find the gestures and attitudes that suit you best. Find strength and repose in beautiful manners. A dignified posture when sitting is an affirmation of inner freedom and harmony. When the body masters its own form, the spirit is free to accomplish more. Cultivate an ideal posture when sitting, for example, and every part of the body will assume its proper place, leaving us free to concentrate on other things.

The body should be considered not as a 'mass' but as an ensemble of expressive gestures and attitudes. More than 'objective' beauty, a person's facial expressions and movement are what make them pleasant or otherwise to look at.

The way we carry ourselves, our smile, our facial expressions, our gaze, are precious gifts. All can be worked on, corrected, improved, for greater harmony. Everyone should try to find the most natural, appropriate gestures for them, the most harmonious way to use their body.

Beauty lies in the texture and tone of the skin, in properly exercised, supple muscles, a slim silhouette, greater delicacy of gesture, fluidity of movement, and dignified posture.

Our daily life is a web of simple, repeated actions. In Japan, these are practised from earliest childhood: sitting down, standing up, washing, chopping vegetables, making a bed, wringing out a cloth, folding a kimono.

We should all learn how to walk, lift heavy objects and express ourselves better verbally: to speak more correctly, and to regulate our flow of words. Voice coaches specialise in teaching people how to moderate the sound of their voice, how to enhance its charm, how to sound appealing, even irresistible!

Everything can be practised and refined. True aesthetes and artists express their essential attitudes in physical form, through their gestures and actions. Training the body in this way can help us progress by refining and preserving our faculties.

When an action is repeated, it becomes anchored deep inside us. Ultimately, it becomes the outward expression of an inner reality, for better or worse. In short, it becomes a habit. Once we have attained our goal, we can stop practising, as when we obtain our driver's licence. Awkward, unattractive gestures can give a false impression of our true identity. This is a shame, when simple practice can often eliminate them altogether. Repetitive exercises are boring and exacting, but they can produce astonishing results.

Freeing the body: sleep and other treatments

THE IMPORTANCE OF GROOMING

'Well-groomed people are the real beauties. It doesn't matter what they're wearing or who they're with or how much their jewellery costs or how much their clothes cost or how perfect their make-up is: if they're not clean, they're not beautiful.'

Andy Warhol

Beauty begins with the basics: good skin, healthy hair, toned muscles and an energetic disposition. For good health, eat properly, take exercise and get enough sleep. Combine a healthy diet with baths, body scrubs and a little exercise, and you'll be in great shape.

A few simple recipes and basic principles, properly applied, can work wonders. The older the recipe, the more effective it is (or it will have been forgotten)!

SCULPT, SCRUB, PURGE, CLEANSE, NOURISH AND ADORN YOUR BODY

'The one luxury was speed, and all that favoured it, the finest horses, the best sprung carriages, luggage as light as possible, clothing and accessories most fitted to the climate. But my greatest asset of all was perfect health.'

Marguerite Yourcenar, *Memoirs of Hadrian*, tr. Grace Frick

No one feels liberated if they are uncomfortable in their own skin, or if their body is not perfectly groomed and cared for.

Grooming frees us from obsessing over our defects. We can forget our concern with our appearance and become more spontaneous, warm, and smiling. Self-assured women with a strong presence are always perfectly groomed. Chipped nail varnish, overly tight or baggy clothes, sweaty skin, bad breath, yellow teeth, lack of sleep and unwashed hair can ruin a day, a trip, an encounter.

A well-made-up person radiates positive energy. Don't be passive – you can change, you can become more radiant. Any time spent on yourself (skin cleansing, a massage or a manicure) will make you more aware of your body and the need to look after it.

BEFORE YOUR BEAUTY TREATMENTS

Clear your bathroom and your head. Faithfully and regularly practised, certain essential beauty rituals and principles will become second nature.

When we take care of our body, we take care of our mind and spirit, and we are better able to take care of others. Everything that happens occurs first in our head. Be positive, extend your knowledge, smile and have confidence!

Equip yourself with a full-length mirror, reliable weighing scales and a small notebook in which to keep a record of your weight, the names of your favourite beauty products and a few beauty recipes (not too many, or you'll never use them all, and feel guilty). Note down any health problems you need to resolve, and the dates of your medical visits. Manage your health and beauty as closely as your finances.

Make an informed distinction between treatments that require the help of a professional (haircuts, teeth whitening, the removal of minor blemishes) and treatments you can carry out yourself (manicure and pedicure, hair masks and facials, massages, etc.).

Apply simple common sense. Many people spend a fortune on diet products but continue to eat too much sugary food. We need to create order and balance in our own minds and lives, starting with a careful examination of the psychological, emotional or clinical factors affecting our behaviour.

Transform your bathroom into your own private beauty institute. Keep it perfectly clean and tidy – a treat for the senses, with everything to hand. Check the contents of your vanity case and keep just a few products of the finest quality. This will bring confidence, pleasure and satisfaction.

2

Minimalist beauty care

Skin, hair and nails

SKIN CARE

Less is more for your skin, too. Most commercially available products do not provide any benefit.

Most importantly of all, avoid junk food. Choose food that will satisfy your health and beauty, not your cravings. The Chinese think of food as medicine.

Remember that junk beauty products are as readily available and harmful as junk food.

To cleanse your skin, use a good-quality gentle soap made with glycerine or honey. Use it every evening to cleanse and/or remove make-up. Dust and other impurities settle in the protective layer of sebum secreted by your skin (this is why many people have a sallow complexion at the end of the day), so careful cleansing is essential: your skin needs to breathe. Ice-cold water is your best asset each morning, when soap is unnecessary. Japanese women tap their face with their fingers one hundred and fifty times each morning to stimulate the circulation and enhance their skin tone.

Next, nourish your skin as dictated by its condition: if the weather is damp, there will be almost no need for moisturiser. Use cotton pads to apply cold tea: the natural oils will protect your skin without blocking pores. If your skin feels tight or dry, simply warm a few drops of oil in the palm of your hand (to aid penetration) and apply. As a rule, foods that are good for your health will be good for your skin, too: olive oil, avocados, sesame seeds, almonds, etc.

Take a moment to massage your face when applying drops of oil: take time to study, understand and practise this daily ritual. Our faces have over three hundred tiny muscles. Properly massaged, they help keep our features and skin toned. The appearance of your skin depends on its elasticity. Be careful not to pull or stretch it with aggressive rubbing or bad habits (resting your cheek in your hand, or your chin on your fists).

Be conscious of your everyday actions: this is vital, as effective beauty rituals depend on your mindset. Loving your skin while you care for it is like talking to a plant when it's watered: the result will be more beautiful. Our skin and hair reflect the health of our organism as a whole, our environment and, above all, our thoughts.

One last tip: the sun is enemy number one for ageing skin. Protect yourself with a hat and sunglasses to avoid extra wrinkles.

DON'T WASTE MONEY ON HARMFUL SKIN PRODUCTS

There are two kinds of nudity: an absence of clothes, and an absence of chemical products on the skin. Get plenty of fresh air, let your skin breathe. Wear lightweight clothes whenever possible. Reactivate your body's energy points daily.

Your skin needs to be cleansed and nourished, but expensive soap, lotions or creams are unnecessary. Resist the lure of the beauty industry – say no to industrial beauty products, lotions and complicated routines. Like your digestive system, whatever you feed your skin is absorbed and passed into the bloodstream. Some cosmetic products can pollute and even poison our systems.

The best skin treatments are a healthy diet, adequate sleep, fresh water and ... happiness. Everything else is secondary. Expensive cosmetics and treatments are unnecessary. Skincare should be confined to deep cleansing, good nutrition and maximum protection. Simplifying your beauty routine can be hard: we are conditioned by magazines and advertising, made to feel guilty if we don't use certain body and beauty treatments, manipulated into believing that the more costly a product, the better its results. But ask any beautifully groomed woman what products she uses and she'll probably answer, 'Oh, hardly anything!'

A YOUTHFUL FACE

Puffy, dark-rimmed eyes are a sign of fatigue and low energy, often related to poor liver function. These symptoms will quickly disappear if you adopt a leaner, healthier diet avoiding spices, meat, salt, sugar and saturated fats. I also like to use vinegar to help clear the skin: drink 50ml of apple vinegar mixed with 150ml water every day for a month. If you do this and adopt a healthier diet focusing on unprocessed foods and fruit and vegetables, you will see miraculous results.

Massage your face with oil, concentrating on the contours of your eye to activate the circulation (three times around, clockwise, starting from the corner of the eye, then three times the other way) but do this gently, do not drag the skin. Next, take a moment for some 'eye gym': drop your chin while looking up, then roll your eyes. Look at yourself often in the mirror. Don't be afraid to confront your own image. This is how you will achieve results.

Repeat certain rituals over time, so that they become ingrained. Health and beauty are impossible without good, regular habits.

SOME HOME-MADE BEAUTY RECIPES

EXFOLIATION

Method 1: In a coffee grinder, whizz small azuki beans to a coarse powder, mix with a teaspoon of water in the palm of your hand then rub over your skin using small, circular movements. Rinse with water.

Method 2: Rub your face for two or three minutes with the inside of a papaya or mango skin: the fruits contain powerful enzymes that dissolve the impurities in the sebum (and body fat, too). Cosmetics manufacturers use them in their products, but in tiny quantities. Wash off with water.

DEEP CLEANSING

Boil two litres of water, add two or three drops of essential oil (lavender, lemon, etc.) and give your face a steam bath to open the pores. Next, apply a home-made face mask: one or two teaspoons of flour mixed with the same quantities of yogurt, lemon, rice wine, and juiced root vegetables. Almost all fresh foods in your refrigerator are therapeutic. Experiment, and see the results for yourself.

FOOD, WATER AND SLEEP

Try to eat only fresh, unprocessed foods.

Drink mineral water – its trace elements are essential. Water is the finest of all beauty products.

Get to bed before midnight and be sure to get six to eight hours sleep per night. Too much or too little sleep is bad for your health.

Introduce soya-based products into your diet: they will help you look and feel younger.

Learn how to recognise and choose medicinal foods: seeds, fruits, fresh herbs.

Wrinkles don't make you look old, but a dull, grey complexion and poor circulation can be very ageing.

Another secret: vinegar. Diluted in a little water, vinegar will dissolve soap deposits on the skin and hair. A bottle of apple vinegar, a gentle soap, a fine quality oil, shampoo and conditioner should be the only products in your bathroom.

FOUNDATION

It's said that once a woman has discovered her perfect foundation cream, she can conquer the world.

Buy a top-quality foundation and make sure its presence on your skin is imperceptible. Apply it very sparingly to the T zone and under the eyes, with the tips of your fingers, but don't rub it in. Applied in a thick uniform layer, it will look unnatural. Remember, any excess product on your skin will block your pores. Here, as always, less is more.

FOR DRY SKIN

Eat half an avocado daily, and mash a teaspoonful of the flesh. Apply this to the face as a mask (I guarantee miracle results). Add a glass of Japanese sake and three drops of essential oil to your bath. Wash your face with water before cleansing with soap. For normal skin, a tiny drop of oil is enough to moisturise. For mixed or greasy skin, the best treatment is . . . nothing at all. Identify the greasy zones first, and use soap on these only, having first blotted them with a soft towel. Warm water (or ice-cold water, in summer) is all you need each morning. Avoid eating wheat-based and dairy products (except yogurt).

YOUR 'UNIQUE OIL'

Find a single, top-quality oil for your face, hair, body and nails. All manufactured creams owe their texture to the presence of glycerine, which blocks the pores and prevents skin from breathing (though glycerine soap is fine providing the skin is thoroughly rinsed). Don't clutter your vanity case, or your bathroom surfaces. Create a space in which to care for your body, and make it as beautiful as possible. Your bathroom should be as pure and clean as the beauty treatments you administer.

Our systems need a drop of oil, inside and out.

INSIDE ...

Supplement your food with a daily, generous spoonful of fine quality, cold-pressed olive oil. This is an essential practice for good health, helping to keep the body supple, and maintain the intestinal wall.

... AND OUT

Our bones become fragile over time, alas, but oil applied to the body is rapidly absorbed and it is believed that it may penetrate to the bones, helping to guard against the fractures so often suffered by older people. Oil massages, practised since antiquity, are not merely a pleasure and a luxury: they are important preventive health treatments, too.

Avocado oil, in particular, is excellent for the body and face. It prevents the formation of tiny wrinkles around the eyes and helps keep the skin elastic and supple. It does not lead to blackheads, and is rich in vitamins B and E. Use it as a hair mask: it will be absorbed into the protective sebum coating the hair shaft, making it more resistant to industrial shampoos.

From time to time (once or twice each month), rub your body all over with a fragrant oil before bathing in hot water. Surprisingly, the oil (not more than a soupspoon) does not float on the water, but is easily absorbed through the skin's dilated pores (a reaction to the hot water). Add some classical music and a scented candle for ultimate relaxation! After your bath, your skin will be smooth and baby-soft.

Oil is the perfect facial cleanser, too. Even stubborn mascara will disappear. Simply pour a little oil into the palms of your hands, then massage your face thoroughly, concentrating on the areas with the most make-up. Next, wet your hands, massage your face again and finally, wash your face with running water (lukewarm or cold, with gentle soap if you prefer). Dry your face: your skin will be soft and clean, with closed pores – no need for moisturising cream or lotion. The perfect, minimalist beauty treatment!

Different oils have different properties – find the one that suits you best. Avocado oil is one of the richest. Mixed with a few drops of a floral essential oil, it leaves a delicious scent on the skin. Try sweet almond oil, often used on babies' skin. Some oils – such as olive oil or sesame oil – have a strong smell, however, and are less pleasant to use.

HAIR

The condition of your hair depends a great deal on your diet: seaweed and sesame seeds are elixirs for the hair.

Don't wash your hair too often, except in humid or hot weather. Use as little shampoo as possible. Dilute it in water in a small bowl, and work up a lather before applying it to the hair: this is the best way to ensure it doesn't coat your hair, even after rinsing, as so often happens. Give your hair a final rinse with clear water and a spoonful of apple vinegar. Learn how to massage the scalp when shampooing, focusing on specific acupuncture points. We tend to neglect the health of our scalp despite the fact that in times of stress, it can contract and prevent the hair from growing properly. 'Unstick' the scalp from the skull by massaging it stiffly with all ten fingers. Lastly, add natural sheen to your clean, dried hair by applying a few drops of your 'unique oil'.

Brush your hair with your head hanging down (this is excellent for blood circulation in the scalp), but do so gently, and never when your hair is too wet. Choose a wooden comb with thick teeth. Despite their long, thick hair, Japanese women never used brushes prior to Westernisation.

Go to your hairdresser regularly. 'Bad hair days' are 'bad mood days' too.

When you visit your hairdresser, never give them carte blanche: explain exactly what you want. Learn to love your hair and respect its natural texture. Properly groomed, natural hair looks far more distinguished than artificial colours and perms, or over-complicated cuts.

Ask your hairdresser to show you how to achieve 'salon' styling yourself: how to hold the dryer and fix grips, what to do from start to finish. Ask for a special appointment so that they have time to show you how to fix a chignon or a messy up-do yourself. If they refuse, find someone more customer-oriented! Your hairstyle affects how your face and figure are perceived. Everyone has at least one hairstyle that's guaranteed to set off their best features.

Above all, if your hair is suitable, let it grow and fix it up in a chignon. A beautiful chignon worn with diamond or pearl earrings and a bright lipstick will make any woman, of any age, look elegant and distinguished. If you have grey or white hairs, resist the temptation to dye them; there is no shame in looking one's age.

OLIVE OR AVOCADO OIL HAIR MASK

Once again, don't clutter up your bathroom and waste precious money on expensive hair treatments that deliver barely satisfactory results.

Warm a small half-cup of olive or avocado oil: use enough for your hair volume, and do not boil.

Apply it to your towel-dried hair and cover with a warm, damp towel to allow it to penetrate. When the towel has dried out, immerse it in warm water and repeat the operation five or six times. Then wash with a gentle shampoo. Your hair will be shinier, and much less dry. As an additional treatment, mix the oil with a fresh egg yolk and a little rum, then soak the hair for 20 minutes. Two or three spoonfuls of mayonnaise are equally effective. Use this home remedy (excellent for restructuring damaged hair) once a week, when you have time.

NAILS

Your nails can make or break your appearance.

Beautifully manicured nails are a magical boost to your morale and the image you project to others.

A few sessions with a professional manicurist will be useful, to learn the correct gestures and procedures. As with your hairdresser, ask as many questions as possible so that you can repeat the treatment at home. Then be your own manicurist! Place all your instruments, towels and a bowl of hot water on a tray, have a good film and a delicious drink ready, switch off your phone and devote yourself body and soul to the twenty precious gems right there at your fingertips.

HOW TO PROCEED

1. File your nails. Find a shape and length of nail to flatter your hands, and keep them that way. For rough skin and callouses, use a good quality, fine emery board on any dry skin.

2. Rub oil into the cuticles to soften them, then let your fingers soak in the bowl of hot water for a quarter of an hour.

3. Gently push back the cuticles with a small boxwood stick soaked in your 'unique oil'. Remove any flecks of dead skin with pincers. If you scrub your nails regularly with a brush, these will reoccur less frequently. A good quality nail brush with hard bristles is absolutely essential.

4. Buff your nails with a polisher.

5. Massage and nourish each nail with your 'unique oil'. Concentrate on the base of the nail, where regrowth occurs. Your nails' two worst enemies are water and nail polish remover, which dry them and make them brittle. A tiny drop of oil at the base of each, once or twice a day, preferably before wetting them, will offer deep-down protection, even if your hands are frequently in contact with water. Wear gloves when cleaning, house-painting or gardening.

6. Wipe the surplus oil away with a tissue (not cotton wool, which will leave threads), then apply one or two base layers of nail polish. When properly applied, nail varnish will actually protect your nails (contrary to popular opinion) and last almost a week. Perfect nails on well-cared-for hands need only a transparent, delicate base colour. For your toes, a whole range of pretty, bright colours are a secret pleasure each time you slip off your shoes.

No more impurities

*Treasure your body, look at it, reconnect it
with your inner self.*

Restore yourself to peak health by changing your daily habits. Begin with a deep-down cleanse: a system loaded with toxins cannot function correctly. Your skin is your health barometer. Its primary function is the elimination of toxins. Your keys to success are water, a body brush, senses on full alert, and real determination.

You have created the body you see in the mirror. The Japanese, Swedes and many other peoples have practised body scrubs for centuries.

In tandem with a balanced diet, a body scrub is one of the most effective beauty and preventive health treatments there is – and one you can have free of charge, no matter where you are.

Experience total cleansing and show a dazzling complexion to the world: use a body brush.

Practise this quick, simple exfoliation ritual. Body brushing helps eliminate dull, grey skin from the elbows and knuckles, knees and heels, from dry cuticles, and patchy, peeling areas. Regularly brushing over a few days will produce spectacular results.

Body brushing is invigorating and energising. It reinforces the immune system, allows the pores to open and breathe, and encourages harder, less brittle nails.

People who do not practise regular body brushing see a gradual deterioration in their complexion as their metabolism slows with age. Body brushing cleanses the lymphatic system, which drains toxins from our tissues. Dry brushing stimulates the expulsion of toxins lodged near the surface of the skin. A third of all waste matter in our body is eliminated through the skin, via the sweat glands (around 400g per day, it is estimated).

In addition, touching our body stimulates the production of hormones that nourish our bloodstream and muscle tissue, nerve cells, glands, hormones and vital organs. Without physical contact to stimulate the secretion of these substances, we experience withdrawal symptoms akin to those of hunger.

Begin your day with a body brush, and experience the benefits for your heart, mind and spirit alike. Body brushing is a ritual, an expression of love. Take your brush with you wherever you go. Do all you can to take care of your body.

Most women exist in 'survival mode'. They think: 'If I could lose 10 kilos . . . If I wasn't so stressed . . . If I slept better at night . . . If I found the love of my life . . .' They are content to survive from day to day, and do nothing to help them create and live the life they dream about. Start by taking care of your body, and much will change. Body brushing helps you to discover a new beauty regime, acquire new habits, develop muscle tone and be more conscious of your body as a whole (diet, make-up, hair). Above all, brushing is a therapeutic treatment. The skin is an emotional organ; each cell retains the memory of past traumas. Medical research has recently proved the existence of a type of memory that is not only cerebral, but cellular. Each cell retains the memory of events, it experiences joy and sorrow, and reacts to changes in our mood. American doctor Christiane Northrup is famous for her research in this field. She explains how massages, for example, can help cells rid themselves of certain 'wounds'. Bathing and brushing can also help the healing process.

Accept and be grateful for your health, beauty and wisdom, and strive to better yourself each day.

HOW TO BODY BRUSH

Brush yourself all over with a body brush for five minutes each day before bathing or showering, or before dressing or getting into bed. You'll feel a wonderful tingling sensation, and if you do it just before you go to bed you'll fall asleep instantly, having scrubbed away the fatigue and travails of the day.

1. Brush your toes and nails, then brush your feet, heels, ankles, calf muscles, knees and thighs (all around), your bottom, stomach, chest, ribs, armpits, the back of your arms, your shoulders. Finally, brush your fingers (especially the cuticles and hands, and brush your neck and ears (take care not to rub too hard).

2. Rinse (by taking a shower).

3. Give yourself an all-over rub with a coarse towel when drying: your skin will glow! Use energetic, circular movements, not forgetting the toes. Concentrate on each part of the body as you rub, always proceeding from the extremities towards the heart, with circular movements.

4. Give yourself an oil massage (half a soupspoon will be enough for the whole body).

BODY CARE KIT

Take a good look at yourself in a long mirror. Note where you have excess fat, dry skin, bruising, blemishes, varicose veins: these are all signs of impurities lodged in your cells. Fewer of all of these will bring enhanced beauty, freedom and power. Your bathroom should be a sanctuary celebrating the pure joy of making yourself look and feel better. Clear your bathroom cupboard of its clutter of chemical products and replace them with:

- A good quality, long-handled bath brush with hog's hair bristles
- A small coarse body towel
- A bar of gentle soap
- A gentle shampoo
- A towel for your hair
- Your 'unique oil'
- A bottle of apple vinegar
- A small bowl in which to dilute the vinegar, froth the shampoo, prepare masks and soak your nails
- A wooden comb

CELLULITE

Commercial anti-cellulite creams are completely ineffective. Exercise, a healthy diet and an element of willpower, on the other hand, will deliver conclusive results. Eat plenty of fresh fruit and vegetables. Avoid industrial, processed foods, drink mineral water and avoid alcohol (an overburdened liver means inefficient detoxification). Walk or run for forty-five minutes daily. Brush your body morning and night. Your cellulite will significantly reduce after six months of effort and perseverance.

Declare war: immerse yourself in a long, hot bath to purify and tone the tissues. Drink hot tea before bathing, to promote detoxification. No need to stick to a draconian diet: simply eliminate certain foods, such as red meat, white flour, sugary foods, alcohol, spices, excessively salty and fried foods, caffeine and tobacco.

WASH YOUR EYES AND NOSE

Did you know that Oriental people wash their eyes and noses?

In Japan, I once spent a day resting at a thermal baths run by an old lady. When I emerged from the bath, she asked if I had washed my eyes thoroughly. Seeing my astonishment, she didn't wait for my answer but went off to fetch a small basin and a pan of hot spring water. She poured the water into a small aluminium bowl and plunged my face into it, telling me to open my eyes and roll them around, even if it stung. After two or three changes of water it won't sting any more, she promised.

I did as she asked, keeping my eyes open and holding my breath for thirty seconds each time. To my astonishment, when I finally lifted my head, I seemed to see more clearly, my eyes felt rested, and the air in my nostrils felt fresher than ever!

I learned that this is a very common practice, especially among Vietnamese Buddhist nuns, for whom physical cleanliness is closely connected to spiritual purity.

TAKE PURIFYING BATHS

As I have already said, in the Zen tradition physical and spiritual cleansing are one and the same. Many hammams are attached to mosques, and regarded as spiritual places whose architecture invites contemplation. Choose a moment alone at home to take your bath. This is one of very few occasions when your senses truly come together: the bath is an enriching experience, purifying body and spirit, and refocusing on your inner self. Bathing is essential for health. It activates the circulation and helps eliminate toxins: perspiring is an essential part of bathing.

After a heavy meal, drink a cup of Chinese Oolong tea, get into a very hot bath, then lie down straight away to start to eliminate toxins through your pores as you perspire.

Dead skin cells are eliminated by brushing prior to bathing, so that soap is unnecessary except for the parts of the body that sweat most. Listen to music as you bathe: soothing strains help the brain secrete a hormone known as ACTH (adrenocorticotropic hormone), noted for its calming, relaxing effect.

A cold shower after a hot bath is sheer delight. The contact of cold water on hot skin contracts the blood vessels and takes the strain off your heart. Your body heat is concentrated and contained, as in a trap. The transition from hot to cold regulates the body temperature by contracting and dilating the blood vessels in the skin. The circulation is stimulated, helping the vital organs to eliminate waste and toxins more effectively.

Savour the contact with the water, listen to the sounds it makes. In Chinese culture, water is the transmitter of the vital energy known as qi. Drink plenty of water, and take a large glass of warm water with lemon juice on waking. Health is not only an absence of sickness: it means possessing and expending vitality, too. A balanced, healthy individual finds meaning, energy and motivation in his or her life. We need vital energy as much as we need food. Be careful not to make physical health an end in itself; keep fit in order to live and work with gusto and enjoyment. Many people underestimate the importance of bathing. A daily bath is essential to good health: it stimulates the metabolism and eases knotted muscles. Bathing is sacred in Japan and Korea alike: few people go to bed without performing the bathing ritual first – one explanation of the robust good health of these peoples.

Fitness without the gym

CREATE YOUR OWN FITNESS REGIME

You don't need a structured, pre-prepared exercise programme to engage in sport or yoga.

It's up to your body to choose what it wants to do, and when, depending your physical condition. It's your sweat, for your body's well-being!

Read fitness magazines and books, talk to the experts, sample classes of all kinds and then create your own perfectly adapted programme. Four one-hour sessions a week is a reasonable average. Make sure you alternate exercises performed indoors on the floor, out of doors, and in water.

Life is characterised by movement and flux. We all need to stay supple to feel well. A willow bends and sways in the wind. It partakes of life with grace and beauty.

Our lifestyles have become so sedentary that some muscles in our body never get a proper workout. Toxins accumulate and stagnate, causing internal poisoning. Muscles have a vital function. When we work them, we reveal their natural beauty. A correctly muscled body radiates vitality even when resting. The posture is correct and undistorted, the movements graceful and fluent, the gestures express a strong, assertive presence. A well-worked and cared-for body retains these qualities well into old age. Mindfully inhabiting our bodies in this way takes introspection and cultivated effort: we need to train our mental and physical faculties alike.

The mind and spirit are not the only gateways to enlightenment: the body offers its own route, too. In our quest for perfection, we learn a great deal about ourselves. This quest is one of the fundamental bases of Oriental disciplines. Take exercise to keep your body young and healthy. Physical exercise eases anxiety, improves your appearance and promotes self-control. It should be part of our daily lives, just like preparing meals and brushing our teeth.

Each time we work our muscles, we teach them to become stronger. Inactivity leads to atrophy, which promotes obesity and depression. Our quality of life depends on how attentive we are to our actions, thoughts and choices. The things we attend to will flourish, and develop.

Try to 'sense' your brain in your legs. Taking part in sport will help you to 'digest' your thoughts. Your body will be awakened, and so will your mind and spirit. You may find yourself struck by the most amazing ideas during exercise. Don't practise sport or yoga with the sole aim of losing weight. Take pleasure in it, like a child running on the beach. Seek out the pleasurable sensations, the energy that exercise brings. People who take regular exercise often seem less stressed, with fewer problems than people who don't. They have a more positive outlook.

Yoga, in particular, enhances beauty – and not only physical beauty. Yoga generates a unique light, charisma and aura all its own.

Cultivate the living resources within you. When you feel relaxed, you will work better, without wasting energy unnecessarily. Try to loosen the corset of tension that stiffens your posture and appearance. This is indispensable if you truly seek to understand and liberate yourself.

Yoga promotes good health. It stimulates your energy, develops the concentration and improves balance. It should be practised regularly, but is richly rewarding: fifteen minutes of concentrated practice daily leads to a more joyful existence.

Physical and mental stress saps our energy reserves. Each time you stretch, savour the sensation and the energy released. Chase out intrusive thoughts and focus on each part of your body in turn. Stopping yoga makes us even more aware of the benefits it brings.

A yogi channels the entire universe and transmits it as positive energy. Awaken this latent energy in your own body: purify it, and concentrate your mental powers. You will gain in intelligence and wisdom, combat negative tendencies of all kinds, and to embrace a more positive outlook. Take beginners' classes for a few months or years: you will soon be able to perform the poses on your own at home. All you need is a mat, a full-length mirror, and some soft music to create your own magical bubble, a world unto itself. You will feel different from the rest of the world; even your appearance will change. Often, after a few weeks of yoga practice, things that seemed impossible at first glance will be achievable, just as when learning a musical instrument, or a language.

EMBRACE DISCIPLINE

Your body is a repository of knowledge and techniques. Remember the tea ceremony, with its focus on the learning of forms? Through discipline, the practitioner achieves release from material comforts and physical laziness, and attains a state of perfect tranquillity. We should also assiduously and consistently devote a portion of our time to meditation, reading, music or walking. These disciplines should be self-imposed, and practised with pleasure and conviction.

In the West, 'discipline' suggests hardship, effort, suffering. In Asia, it is understood a priori as beneficial to the body, mind and spirit. The geniuses of the European Renaissance used repetitive practice and technical exercises to elevate painting and sculpture to new heights of creativity, celebrating the culture of 'mind and hand'.

Imitation and emulation are important when acquiring new skills and faculties. Eventually, one day, they become second nature: we are no longer copying, but have made the skill our own. By practising discipline in the service of beauty, we find a thousand ways to perfect ourselves and become more radiant.

Five minutes of concentrated discipline can deliver better results than forty-five minutes of superficial dabbling. When we know the power of discipline, we understand its benefits more fully. Set yourself small personal targets and challenges: eat little, get up at dawn, take a cold shower. Make them part of your lifestyle. You will develop greater strength of character and stamina for the things that matter. The twilight, peace and calm of early morning help transform these ascetic disciplines into precious rituals.

PRACTISE PERFECTION

'Perfection is not doing exceptional things, but doing
ordinary things exceptionally well.'

Japanese proverb

Avoid tedium by transforming ordinary tasks into rituals. Everything can be accomplished with aesthetic flair, even chores.

Choose a solitary occupation, like washing the floor, scrubbing pans, walking in a forest, taking a bath or exercising. Try to focus on your activity to the exclusion of all else, engage in it conscientiously, see it through to completion. Don't hurry, and don't think about anything else. Be content to partake of this activity, here and now. Rediscover the riches inherent in actions or gestures that have become a part of your very being; bring to them the same freshness and enthusiasm as you did the very first time.

Practise focusing your concentration on all that you are. Strive continually to surpass yourself, to do things better than ever. Be conscious of everything you touch. Accomplish your morning ablutions as if they were a specific exercise; proceed with care and order. We have so much more to learn . . .

Films by the Japanese director Ozu show us how to respect each of our tasks, each action, however insignificant. When his characters perform an action, however ordinary, they become completely absorbed in what they are doing or saying, putting all other preoccupations from their minds. Their presence becomes suffused with meaning, and daily activities are seen and experienced as an expression of formal harmony. The body is understood as an entity in its own right.

The best way to ensure your everyday gestures remain supple and 'fluent' is to own only things that are beautiful and useful. They are our source of grace. Act slowly and gracefully, but practise swiftness, too. Approach each moment as an opportunity for new discoveries.

3

Eat less but better

Eating too much

EVERY TIME WE PUT ON WEIGHT, WE DIE A LITTLE

'Every time we put on weight, we die a little. We turn our backs on elegance, pleasure, gracefulness, sveltesse, even our true looks. We lose our health itself. Putting on too much weight constricts the functioning of essential organs (the heart, kidneys and liver), just as it restricts movement, deforms the body, results in a heavy gait, and prevents us from keeping active. Putting on weight means saying goodbye to life's pleasures, losing our looks and ageing before our time. To lose weight is be rejuvenated, to rediscover our youthful silhouette, to be born again into the joy of living.'

Article from a women's magazine, 1948

Health comes with awareness. We live in a society that has too much to eat, where obesity is a growing problem. Obesity is a disease of acquisitiveness: the accumulation of sensory pleasure, and food. We want more of everything, all the time, leading to stress – the primary cause of death in the West. The key symptoms of stress are linked to faults in our human make-up.

We need to treat people, not diseases.

Too much or too little, too soon or too late: these are the factors that govern disease and healing. To obtain a natural balance, we need to eliminate physical and mental toxins.

SELF-ESTEEM: THE ONLY WAY TO SLIM

More than her husband, children or friends, a woman's most intimate relationship is with her own body. She owes her existence to it, her feelings, her capacity to give and to nourish others. If her body is not functioning well, it's a safe bet that nothing else will, either. Losing weight is impossible unless we also enhance our self-esteem in a thousand and one small ways. Dietetics is a philosophy, a body of wisdom. Living well means looking for the meaning inherent in each moment of life; eating less is one of the most important ways of simplifying our life.

The following tips should only be followed if you have no specific health problems. They should in no way replace or override the advice of your doctor, but are based on my own sensible, informed experiments and experiences. I honestly believe that there is no such thing as a one-size-fits-all diet. The only universally applicable weight loss technique is the elimination of all negative thoughts: we cannot enjoy good health and move forward with positivity if we feel neither love nor joy.

A LIGHTER BODY, A LIGHTER LIFE

'The worst disease is scorn of one's own body.'

Montaigne

Take care of your body. Take it out and about. Smile. Treat yourself to fragrant baths and fine, comfortable clothes. Rediscover the marvellous, simple pleasure of moving, stretching, walking, dancing . . . Enjoy your campaign to achieve a more balanced life. Liberating the body takes discipline. To stay slim, eat frugally. The effort, and the results obtained, will deliver unimagined satisfaction.

A poor diet can have serious consequences, draining our vital energy little by little.

Eat lighter meals for a longer life. Eating little is my golden rule. If you fail to respect it, your body will struggle to assimilate even the finest quality food. Food of poor nutritional value leads to a lack of energy, more visits to the doctor, a higher intake of medicines. You will study less effectively, feel muddle-headed, lead an emptier, less fulfilling life and career. Overly rich food demands constant effort to digest and assimilate it. Poor diet can increase the risk of conditions such as cardiovascular disease, joint problems and types of cancer, so take care to rid yourself of impurities.

GOODBYE FAT

Carrying excess weight places strain on the knees, hips and spinal column. Eventually, excess weight will disrupt the systems regulating our fat and sugar intake, in some cases leading to Type 2 diabetes and high levels of cholesterol in the blood. People start to look plump when they have too much body fat compared to their muscle mass. Develop your muscles, and you will burn fat more quickly.

In the past, people's fat reserves saw through 'lean' times of the year, until the earth was able to feed them again. Today, Western societies eat too much poor quality food.

Lose body fat and say goodbye to migraines, back pain, fatigue and apathy. Eating little keeps the digestive tract clear and accelerates the combustion of energy and the elimination of waste. Resisting temptation is ultimately liberating.

Mealtimes: simple quality

A WOODEN BOWL

Some people remain in excellent health well into old age thanks to their eating habits. Himalayan people eat rice, two or three small fish grilled over a fire, and vegetables from their garden. In China, centenarians live on stone-ground rice congee with one or two added vegetables, sautéed in a wok.

I eat my everyday meals from a fine wooden bowl. It holds the right amount of food for my physique and physiology (remember, the stomach is said to be roughly the size of your fist). My bowl helps me to limit my choices: a little rice, a soupspoon of green vegetables, a small piece of fish (or an egg, or tofu), seasoned with sesame seeds, herbs and spices; a hearty soup in winter, a mixed salad in summer.

Apart from special celebrations, Oriental people often eat a simple bowl of rice, soup or noodles at mealtimes.

For Oriental mystics seeking to live by their ethics and ideals, the wooden bowl symbolises poverty and frugality. It is a quiet statement of opposition to the excesses and opulence of Western society, achieved at the expense of the lives of millions of exploited fellow humans.

EAT BEAUTIFULLY, IN FINE SURROUNDINGS

When a dish is perfectly prepared and well presented, in a delightful setting, we don't need large portions in order to feel satisfied.

A few bites will be enough. Quality is nourishing in so many ways!

Living life to the full means finding meaning in every moment. If you eat in ugly surroundings, you will compensate your craving for beauty with an excess of food. Dress for dinner (or lunch, or break-fast): change into fresh clothes, brush and refix your hair, freshen up. You'll feel better in yourself, and eat less. Try to serve your meals as aesthetically as possible: not hurriedly on a corner of the kitchen table! Avoid plates and cutlery in paper or plastic. Banish these from your table, and life will look better straight away. Past generations of Japanese ate off nothing but handmade ceramics, and wooden or lacquered tableware: I believe this is why care was always taken to serve the humblest vegetable with unparalleled aesthetic flair. Since the Second World War and the development of mass industry, children have grown up surrounded by plastic, and no longer distinguish between 'base' and 'noble' materials. Plastic belongs nowhere except inside the refrigerator. These may seem like insignificant, pointless details, but they enrich our daily lives, and remind us that everyday life should be as pleasurable as possible. Feeling sated depends on the quality of the food we eat, not its quantity. The quality of our surroundings, and our own inner life, are vital too.

It's said the Essenes (an ascetic Judaic sect of desert dwellers in ancient times) bathed before each meal then gathered to eat in small sanctuaries, after dressing in ceremonial clothes. They served themselves once only and ate from small bowls.

Serve your guests the finest asparagus tips, a grilled fish and wholemeal bread fresh from the oven, followed by a perfectly mature cheese: no one will object to the simplicity of the meal. We have become too forgetful of what constitutes healthy food. We dress our food up too much, because it has become 'denuded' and robbed of its natural flavour.

In my opinion, we should follow the model of dietary hygiene set by a religious group, the Seventh-Day Adventists. Their religion forbids them from eating foodtstuffs that have been chemically treated. Everything must be 100 per cent organic. It goes without saying that there are very few sick people in Adventist communities . . .

The Shakers, too, venerated the supreme luxury of meals composed of the freshest, home-grown food, and used no seasoning other than herbs – a close relative of *nouvelle cuisine*.

EAT SLOWLY AND DELICATELY

Counting calories, depriving ourselves of food and buying expensive 'medicine-foods' are unnecessary, and symptomatic of compulsive behaviour. Instead, we should practise mindfulness, and pay attention to what we think and feel.

Eating well means eating slowly and delicately, showing respect for the food and for our body. Controlling the way we eat is the route to controlling our weight. Breathe before each morsel. Breathe out your stress and negativity. Eating slowly and savouring your food go hand in hand.

I would summarise my daily dietary needs as follows: three handfuls of vegetables, two pieces of fruit, six portions of bulk food (bread, rice or pasta), one small quantity of protein (fish, tofu, eggs or meat), plus a handful of pulses (beans, lentils, peas) twice a week. As a general rule, 200g of rice, bread or pasta and 100g each of protein (fish, meat, tofu) and vegetables are enough. Individual meals should not exceed the volume of your fist, or an average grapefruit. The main bulk of our diet should be comprised on plant-based foods – vegetables and fruit, wholegrain and unrefined cereals, nuts and seeds, beans and pulses combined with only small quantities of meat and fish.

With these simple rules, you'll spend less time preparing and cooking your food, with the exception of special occasions and annual 'holidays'.

In ancient Japanese culture, the kitchen was a sacred space, dedicated to the preparation of foods designed to promote spiritual advancement. Japanese people see mealtimes as generators of fresh life and thoughts. Even today, the only foodstuff they eat to feel sated is rice, often served at the end of a meal. For the rest, each morsel is savoured and nibbled from the tips of their chopsticks, in the knowledge that a true sense of what is good, and an awareness of the true value of discretion, come only with a certain asceticism.

KITCHEN EQUIPMENT

Nourishment doesn't come solely from eating. Preparing and cooking food, presenting it, and welcoming friends and family to a shared meal are nourishment for the soul. Relish the immense pleasure of washing, cutting and steaming vegetables. Choose the best possible basic equipment, keep your kitchen spotlessly clean and unleash your imagination.

MY BASIC KIT

- A good, well-sharpened knife
- A chopping board
- A measuring tumbler that will double as a sauce bowl
- A small grill-plate (easy to take out and store)
- A small cooking pot for rice and casseroles
- A wok and a bamboo steaming basket
- A sieve
- A multi-function grater/slicer
- Three stackable saucepans with removable handles
- Three ultralight mixing bowls
- A dozen white tea towels
- A pair of kitchen shears
- A Pyrex tart dish
- A Pyrex cake mould
- Spatulas, ladles

Keep all of these utensils on a shelf above your kitchen sink, so that everything is to hand when cooking. Avoid unnecessary to-ing and fro-ing and work, and clean up as you go along. Your kitchen should be clean and tidy before you sit down to eat.

Eat to detox: tips and reminders

CLEANSING YOUR GUT

In the nineteenth century, doctors invariably prescribed a 'lavage' before any treatment. The practice was mocked for many years, but methods such as these are being rediscovered today, in more modern forms. The only difference is that today they are performed in beauty establishments, as part of a preventive health regime, or as 'cosmetic' treatments (for weight loss or an enhanced complexion). Don't ignore the ill effects of constipation: it can increase the risk of other problems like diverticular disease, and will delay the elimination of toxins from the digestive tract, which can increase the risk of cancer.

Constipation is often chronic when travelling. Irritation, stress and anxiety can also affect bowel function.

Ensure that your food contains enough fibre to form healthy stools. Some doctors recommend 30g of fibre per day, in the form of wholegrain cereals such as wholemeal bread or brown rice, beans and pulses, seaweed (*kanten*, found in most good health food stores and used as a gelling agent, is excellent), sweet potatoes, soaked prunes, fresh fruit and vegetables. Your intestine, not your stomach, digests your food. Chew thoroughly so that the enzymes in your saliva predigest what you eat, lightening the strain on your digestive tract.

FASTING: AN ANCIENT TRADITION

The practice of fasting has existed since ancient times, for dietary and spiritual purposes alike. Short-term fasting does not deprive the body of elements essential for overall health: the practice even exists in the animal kingdom. It is performed as a rite in many countries, and costs nothing whatsoever.

After fasting, the body needs less food and is satisfied with smaller portions. You will feel leaner and more energetic, and work with greater gusto. Body and mind alike are released from the endless, negative cycle of wanting, demanding, desiring, envying. Fasting helps us to recover a more balanced, ordered, uncomplicated approach to food.

Anyone embarking on a fast for three days or more, or anyone with a pre-existing medical condition, should seek advice from a medically qualified doctor. Fasting is not suitable for pregnant women.

PSYCHOLOGICAL PREPARATION FOR FASTING

Small, successive fasts are easier, psychologically and practically, than longer fasts, which require a certain amount of training and experience. Fasting is a practice that needs to be worked at. Begin with a fast of half a day, then twenty-four hours, then forty-eight hours over a quiet weekend, or on holiday. Seek advice from a nutritionist or dietician if you are considering a longer fast. Mini-fasts, one day per week, or two consecutive days per month, should be a regular part of your dietary programme.

Fasting needs determination, conviction and a responsible approach. I believe that successful fasting will help evacuate the toxins accumulated from food, alcohol, tobacco or stress from the cells where they are lodged.

Before you start, remember that interrupting a fast prematurely may do more harm than not fasting. Your stomach may have shrunk, and cut its production of gastric juices. If you start eating again without proper preparation, you might be unable to digest your food properly.

During your fast, drink plenty of water, get out in the sunshine and avoid problematic situations. Prepare your fast as a rite, and anticipate the joys and benefits it will bring. A fast will deliver no benefits if you force yourself, or if you undertake it solely in the interest of losing weight. Remember first and foremost that a fast is designed to energise your system, cleanse the body and improve morale.

Fasting requires psychological preparation. At first, try fasting for a weekend, three or four times a year, to 'clear out' your system. Fasting is useless if it is not undertaken in a spirit of restraint and respect for the body. Its success depends essentially on your state of mind at the outset.

During your fast, drink plenty of mineral water. Water can help the body eliminate toxins. Use an attractive glass and order two cases of sparkling water. Gradually, your appetite will disappear. If you drink fruit juice, your stomach will be stimulated and continue to demand food.

Under normal conditions, food 'titillates' your palate, which continues to savour its last meal, or anticipate the next. When nothing is eaten – and only as part of a full fast – the sensory memory of food disappears and fasting itself becomes a pleasure.

The body begins to draw on its own reserves and eliminate its own excess. Fasting helps the body to burn off excess fat and eliminate toxins. Energy that is no longer being expended on digestion is diverted to the process of cleansing, extracting and gradually expelling toxins lodged deep in the cells. The work of cleansing begins. Hippocrates warned long ago that 'by feeding ourselves, we feed our diseases'.

DURING AND AFTER THE FAST

Begin by taking a vegetable-based laxative (they are not habit-forming). This will help you to feel the first effects of your cleansing process. Next, around midday, if you begin to feel tired or weak, take a cold shower and give yourself a massage. Remind yourself that you are now living off your own fat reserves. Anything other than very gentle exercise like stretching is not recommended while fasting.

These small victories will boost your confidence and prepare you for future challenges. Don't try to look too far ahead: even thinking about food can make you feel hungry. Try to think about something else: anticipate the pleasure of wearing more fetching clothes, experiencing enhanced self-control, moving with a lighter, more supple body, saying goodbye to irritating small aches and pains.

Replenish your resources in as many other ways as possible: read, meditate, listen to music. Don't stay in bed. The busier you are the better.

The post-fast period is as important as the fast itself. Don't return to your old dietary habits, and certainly not straight away. On the first day after fasting, drink a small glass of fruit juice diluted with water, and a glass of undiluted juice in the evening. On the second day, eat fruit, and a yogurt with salad in the evening. Finally, on the third day, resume eating small quantities of cereals (for example, a slice of wholemeal bread at lunchtime, and another in the evening, with salad and a soup). Chew as thoroughly as possible, and eat slowly. A few bites will be enough for these first meals. You can return to normal eating on the fourth day.

FAST IN ORDER TO ...

- Lose weight (it's the quickest way)
- Feel better physically and in terms of your morale
- Look and feel younger
- Give your system a rest
- Cleanse the body
- Improve digestion
- Brighten the eyes
- Cleanse your complexion
- Freshen your breath
- Sharpen your thought processes
- Rediscover the best eating habits
- Acquire enhanced self-control
- Slow down the ageing process

- Normalise your cholesterol level
- Remedy insomnia and tension
- Live with greater intensity
- Teach your body to consume only what it needs

How to be hungry

Adopt a pace of life that suits you perfectly. Choose foods that satisfy your body's needs (fish, fresh fruit and vegetables, aromatic herbs, quality vegetable oils, 100g of grilled meat once or twice a week) rather than your own cravings. Too many people eat because they feel anxious, or are bored. Stress and a fast-paced lifestyle are our enemies in modern society. If we live too hard and too fast, certain body tissues degenerate more quickly. Learn to take your time, avoid stress, say 'no', and prepare excellent, simple food. Learn how to eliminate negative influences, too. Food is not your enemy, but your most effective medicine.

Eat when you are hungry. Savour each mouthful.

Stop eating when you no longer feel hungry.

In an ideal world, we would all emulate the animal kingdom and eat only when we are hungry, not at fixed times dictated by social convention. On average, babies take around six 'mini-meals' per day, three or four hours apart.

Learn to eat only when your stomach tells you it's hungry, not because it's 'time', or because you're feeling at a loose end in the kitchen, tired between chores, eager to 'reward' yourself after a stressful day at work, feeling 'blue', or red with anger, or green with envy.

This may seem simple, but it takes an effort of mindfulness to exercise brain functions that have become atrophied through misuse. First, we need to identify the sensation of 'hunger' and the feeling of having 'had enough to eat'. We must learn, too, to distinguish between what our body needs us to eat, and what our cravings dictate. When you see a tempting cake, ask yourself: 'Which do I prefer, that cake, or a body I feel comfortable with?' Lastly, learn to properly taste and appreciate your food. The body is a very finely tuned instrument that loves to be taken care of. It possesses its own system of self-regulation: we just need to know how to activate it.

Hunger may be felt one day, but not the next. The body and its demands vary according to a range of factors. If we can't predict when we will need to empty our bowels, then we can't predict, either, when we will feel hungry. There are days when a small meal at 4 p.m. may be all we need, others when we feel hungry as soon as we wake up. Why, then, do we force our bodies to submit to a preset timetable of meals? The freedom to eat only when you are hungry will encourage the freedom to say 'no' to any food you don't want.

DEGREES OF HUNGER

1.   Absolutely ravenous (to be avoided, because you will throw yourself on any food you can find).
2.   Too hungry to care about what you eat.
3.   Seriously hungry: you need to eat right away.
4.   Moderately hungry: you could wait a while longer.
5.   Slightly hungry: (you're not really hungry, in fact).
6.   Sated and relaxed after a meal.
7.   Slightly uncomfortable, feeling 'heavy' and sleepy.
8.   Really uncomfortable, and bloated.
9.   Stomach ache.

The amount of food you need to eat to feel satisfied is the same as the true size of your stomach.

But don't let yourself feel hungry for too long: your stomach will secrete acid juices that attack the stomach wall. The result? Excess fat!

Our daily appetite, the one that pushes us to eat between one and three times a day (if not more), is not stimulated by the need to replace our body's depleted reserves. In reality, most of us eat far more than we need.

We eat because we need to alter our physiological rhythm. It's well known that the first sip of morning coffee is the best, the only one we truly savour. So-called 'peckish' feelings are merely contractions or gastric spasms. Many people believe that the sensations we describe as 'peckishness' are in fact physical expressions of a desire for comfort, love or beauty to compensate for stress, fatigue, sorrow or boredom.

Eating when we are not hungry destabilises the system: learn to avoid it. This takes effort, concentration and personal commitment. Start tomorrow morning: wait for hunger to declare itself, and enjoy the prospect of food. Your stomach will let you know when you are truly hungry. This advice is of course difficult to follow when we are constrained by specific timetables, but with a little ingenuity and foresight, we can work miracles. Prepare small, diet-appropriate, 'snacks' in advance: a rice ball stuffed with tuna and cucumber wrapped in a salad leaf, a wholemeal sandwich with half a slice of ham, a banana, etc.

A tip: when you really feel like snacking on something, but aren't actually hungry, take a small teaspoon of chutney and let it melt in the mouth. Try to identify the five tastes that are said to make up everything we eat: salt, sour, sweet, bitter and umami.

Our hunger is more often in our minds than in our bodies!

DRINKS

Did you know that a can of non-diet soft drink contains the equivalent of twelve lumps of sugar?

To regulate our thirst, we must first of all avoid foods that are either too salty or too sweet. Eating lots of salty food will make you feel thirsty, and sugary drinks will cause your glucose levels to spike and crash. Drinking too much carbonated liquid causes the body to lose calcium, which will increase the risk of osteoporosis.

Drinking fizzy, sugary or alcoholic drinks during mealtimes is a mistake, therefore. I prefer to drink nothing at all while I eat, but many people will object to a table set without glasses. 'What about wine,' you may ask? There are other pleasures in life! No traditional Asian culture drinks with its meals. The Japanese take tea fifteen minutes after a meal, and it should be noted that glasses were unknown in their culture before Westernisation.

Avoiding 'acid' foods (especially sugar and white flour) will prevent excessive thirst. Sugar and salt encourage the body to retain fluids, in order to neutralise their effect.

Drinking between meals is recommended, however. Constipation results from inadequate hydration, especially in older people.

Remember, too, that alcohol, like tobacco, hardens the blood vessels, accelerating the ageing process.

VINEGAR MAGIC

This is my own method to lose extra kilos: take a teaspoon of apple vinegar, and a teaspoon of honey each morning in a glass of hot or ice-cold water. The vinegar is said to eliminate excess proteins, and has all the properties of fresh apples. It can dissolve toxins trapped in our joints, contribute potassium and help the body stay supple.

EAT SIMPLE, DIET-CONSCIOUS FOODS

Rice is the only ideal accompaniment to everything. Combined with pulses, peas and beans, it contributes valuable, health-giving nutrients. Eaten with salad in summer or a winter soup of two or three different vegetables, with a little fish or meat, this makes an excellent lunch and a simple, balanced, hearty, nourishing, economical, non-fattening supper.

These are the only rules you need:

- Eat only fresh, and wholemeal or wholegrain foods. (Avoid processed 'diet' foods, faddy 'miracle' ingredients, frozen food and, of course, tinned foods.)
- Eat dessert only occasionally.
- Take cold food and drinks at room temperature, never straight from the refrigerator.
- Don't eat between meals.
- Eat only one type of protein per day.
- Eat food as soon as you have prepared it.
- Eat fats in moderation and choose heart-friendly fats like

those found in olive oil, nuts and seeds. Minimise animal and vegetable fats (butter, margarine, fatty meats, lard). Choose only the finest cold-pressed oils.

- Avoid salt as much as sugar.
- Favour steaming or parcel-steaming in the oven.

Above all, don't moralise. Enjoy your meals and think nothing further of it. Let your friends eat whatever they like, don't lecture them about food and what constitutes a good diet. It's difficult to achieve perfect food combinations, especially when you are eating alone. But we should always aim for this when choosing ingredients. Most importantly, eat only the finest quality products, in small quantities, and let your friends and family know that there are other ways of enjoying time together, beyond sitting for hours around a table.

POSITIVE THINKING AND MATERIALISATION

Structure your thoughts each day. Hour by hour, you can generate your own radiant health, success and happiness based on the ideas, beliefs and situations you rehearse in the studio of your mind. Remember, putting thoughts into action takes vision: without it, you will lack direction.

You can conjure anything at all in your thoughts, and the more powerful they are, the more they will motivate you to attain your goals. You will become the physical materialisation of your own ideal image: a person radiating vitality, agility and health. You can choose to become whoever you want to be. *You* have that power.

You are capable, for example, of transforming your compulsive appetite into an irresistible desire to possess a slim, youthful body. Eat little and maintain your ideal weight, lead a balanced life, enjoy better health and more rewarding relationships with others: this will impact your mindset as naturally and fully as your vital functions.

NO SELF-CONTROL NEEDED

Imagine reaching one of your goals, and allow your subconscious to truly experience what it feels like: the objective becomes all the more tempting, and you feel more motivated than ever. For many people, willpower alone is not enough for success. What matters is their very real desire to attain a goal, and the way they set about it. All the willpower in the world will be useless, if you have nothing to apply it to.

Willpower is impossible to sustain on a permanent basis. This is why, as soon as we finish a weight-loss diet, we regain weight. But if our subconscious is perfectly conditioned, we can eat whatever we want. Even if we eat too much one day, our mind will tell us the next day: 'Everything's OK, but now, don't eat for a while.' Our appetite will 'lay low' quite naturally for a day or two, while the surplus calories burn off.

If you are carrying too much weight right now, you may tell yourself that this is simply how things are, and always will be. But if you remember a time when things were different, when you weighed less, you will be able to envisage a different future, in which things will be different again. Your determination and hope will be reborn. Projecting yourself into the future in order to experience your goals is an ancient technique.

SUGGESTIVE VISUALISATIONS

Our mind functions in pictures. We don't remember what we ate in words, but in images. Practise visualising healthy, delicious food. At a drinks reception, you'll find yourself reaching automatically for a fruit juice cocktail rather than the *petits fours*. Anxious feelings about your diet will no longer be the subtext to your conversations.

Visualise foods that you know deliver energy, a healthy complexion, beautiful hair. Like dried figs, a mixed tofu salad, a bowl of seeded pomegranates, a sesame-seed biscuit . . .

YOUR PERFECT IMAGE

The real you is there inside, not in the image you offer to the world through your personality. Close your eyes, relax, take your time, then visualise your ideal image, life-sized. Make it exactly as you wish. Enter the body you have created and see how it feels. Reassure yourself that this is indeed the person you want to become. We can't become taller, or shorter, or alter the breadth of our shoulders, or the length of our legs, but we can create a lively, true self-image. Visualise the lifestyle you want. Feel your energy, your vitality, your lightness, your appearance down to the tiniest details (jewellery, make-up, shoes, hair). This is *your* real you. The body you have today will gradually mould to the shape of the image you have visualised.

Now imagine the number you want to see appear on your scales; this is your ideal weight. Your subconscious knows this. The images you have visualised will command your subconscious to transmit it to your body. Generate a sense of self-love, a sense of very strong, inner conviction that you deserve the ideal image you have created. Ask this visualised person to help you lose the kilos that are holding you prisoner, to advise you, and grant you determination, perseverance, good sense. Ask them to reflect *your* true self back at you, as if in a huge mirror, whenever you need it. The image will send you the message you need.

DAILY PRACTICE

Repeat this visualisation, changing nothing, for twenty-one consecutive days, always after taking a moment to relax. You are imprinting a model on your brain. Once the model has become clear and precise, your body will be forced to conform. The body only does what the subconscious dictates. The subconscious does not distinguish between a real experience and an imaginary one. Try to preconstruct the sensation of being inside the 'new me'. But don't tell anyone about your aims. Having to explain what you're doing to people who are not aware of these techniques, and who may doubt their effectiveness, will dilute your energy.

Above all, trust your 'inner me'. Most people eat because they feel anxious. This is why you must visualise the image you desire, and not that of a person torturing themselves at the gym, or suffering a tiny, diet-sized meal.

Visualisation is an exercise through which you can become more and more skilled at realising your hopes and dreams.

We are all prisoners of our psyche. And so we need to programme our subconscious in order to liberate ourselves from it. If you see yourself as a large person, substitute that image with a slim person.

Even a body that has never been svelte can become so. As in so many fields, you will only get what you have chosen to obtain. And so you must enter the correct data into your subconscious, if you want to take the right decisions. Your body will respond to whatever the subconscious dictates.

Our subconscious knows exactly how our body functions, far better than doctors or even we ourselves. It's up to our subconscious to dictate our weight, our ideal body, and the decisions we need to take to that end: not magazines, our friends and family or even our own feelings.

A correctly programmed subconscious is far stronger than willpower in a situation of conflicted choices. Words and images function as effectively as actual molecules to stimulate our vital processes. A wounding word is more difficult to forgive than an act of physical violence. The spectacle of an accident is far more traumatising than any verbal account of the same thing.

Fixed aims, diets, information, exercise . . . Everything contributes to 'upload' the correct data to our mental 'hard drive', including the psychological reasons for our overeating.

Our subconscious controls our appetite. Set yourself a precise goal, and you will shed kilos as a result. Write the weight you are aiming for on a piece of paper. You have the means to reach your goal.

WORK ON YOUR AFFIRMATIONS

Collect your own affirmations – your favourite quotations, phrases that have touched you – and assemble your own personal treasure chest.

Repeat to yourself:

Right now, I am on a path leading to my goal: my ideal body already exists inside me. I swear to do all in my power to reach it as quickly as possible: eat well, take exercise, choose healthy foods, improve my environment.

Whatever happens, I will commit to my goal and allow nothing to stand in my way. This perfect image exists within me, and it will remain there for ever. I will be a charismatic person, drawing to me the things I need to make its coming possible.

The ideal weight for my frame is here inside me, I feel wonderful and I am beautiful. I know that small portions of food are enough, and I am delighted by the idea. I clearly see myself saying 'no' to empty calories, and I love the person I see in the mirror. I can already see the person I will become. I love myself unconditionally.

Visualisations and affirmations go hand in hand. The best way to inscribe images on the subconscious is to enter into a state of relaxation close to sleep, make as little effort as possible, and conceive of an idea.

Condensing this idea into a simple phrase will make it easier to memorise when you repeat it. It should come with no effort, by the intervention of no mental force.

Short phrases hold the attention more easily. They are imprinted more readily on the subconscious. They are less tiring than long paragraphs. Without a book to rely on, they are easier to remember.

The surest way to correct faulty thinking is the repetition of concise, constructive, harmonious thoughts. New mental habits will emerge as a result. Your mindset is the seat of your habitual conduct.

For twenty-one days, repeat a list of affirmations morning and night, until they are profoundly anchored in your make-up. They will generate positive feelings and guide you through life without testing your willpower. These affirmations and visualisations are your guardians, your protectors. They will underpin all your decisions and choices, and play an essential role in your life.

LIST OF SUGGESTIVE AFFIRMATIONS

Read this list through from start to finish, or in sections, as often as possible: in the bath, listening to music, before going out with friends, on the way to work. Keep it to hand in your bag, or posted to your phone, and try to memorise passages whenever you can.

HOW TO EAT: QUALITY NOT QUANTITY

- An empty stomach clears the head, cleanses the spirit and feels pleasant.
- The surroundings in which we eat are as important as our food.
- Crash diets are dangerous: they encourage compulsive behaviour.
- Food is only a problem when it is not chosen and eaten correctly. Rice, pasta or bread once a day is enough.
- Fatty foods make me feel thirsty.
- Hot food is more satisfying than cold food.

- Eating from a single bowl is the best way to control portions.
- I can allow myself one or two bites of even the most fattening food.
- I will only eat foods that are unprocessed or unrefined.
- I am glad that my stomach is resting and not constantly digesting.
- I will chew my food until it is liquefied, and drink in small sips.
- I will distinguish thirst from hunger.
- I will eat at home as often as possible.
- Fresh herbs are friends worth getting to know!
- No mediocre food: we eat more to compensate for the lack of taste.

DIET

- Avoid sugar, salt and alcohol as much as possible.
- Good sources of energy are brown rice, sweet potatoes and potatoes.
- Good sources of protein are tofu, fish, walnuts, hazelnuts, almonds, etc.
- Salt, white flour, sugar and chemical products should be avoided as much as possible.
- Empty calories like sugar and alcohol don't add anything beneficial to the diet.
- Prepare meat, fish and vegetables as simply as possible.
- When hungry, eat slow-burning carbs: a slice of wholemeal bread, spread very thinly with honey, or you could try oatcakes with hummus.

- It is much better to get all the vitamins and minerals you need from food rather than rely on supplements.
- Sugar leads to sugar cravings, salt to salt cravings, alcohol to alcohol cravings.
- Most types of alcohol are a rich source of sugar, which is transformed . . . into fat!
- Vitamin-poor food makes a vitamin-deprived body.
- You will forget the taste of sugar and salt after two or three months, but never the untainted taste of good food.

SELF-CONFIDENCE

- I am beautiful, I am happy, I am light, I am me.
- I am self-confident and enjoy my own company.
- Beauty begins when you accept yourself.
- Each success gives me faith in the next.
- I gave into temptation yesterday, but I can compensate today.
- I can be slim, even if I have never been slim before.
- I can materialise my ideal image.
- I can be as beautiful and slim as I wish.
- I can improve my health by looking at myself in the mirror and loving what I see.
- I can be beautiful without looking like anyone else.
- I like myself the way I am, and I always will.
- If I love my body, my body will love me back.
- My subconscious is in charge of my body.
- There's a radiant person full of vitality inside me.

- There are at least ten ways I could be more myself.
- Self-confidence and self-control are two different things. I trust my body.

WILLPOWER

- If I choose what I want to eat, I can also choose what I don't want to eat.
- I will set myself a goal and commit to reaching it.
- I will swap my compulsion to overeat for a determination to get slim.
- Only I can control my weight.
- I need principles because my spirit doesn't always know what it truly wants.
- My body will tell me when it's hungry. I don't have to think ahead about food.
- A slim figure is my reward for frugality.
- I should feel energised and light after a meal, not tired or sleepy.

TIMING

- Eating is only truly pleasurable when I'm hungry.
- To boost my metabolism, six small meals are better than two big ones.
- I may feel hungry one day and not the next.
- I must always ask my body what it wants before eating.
- I should move around for twenty minutes after a meal (not lie on the sofa).

- Fasting is a planned activity and should not be confused with skipping meals.
- I will eat nothing for three hours before going to bed: my stomach needs to finish digesting before sleep.
- Fasting is an art to be cultivated.
- Peckish feelings will always pass, real hunger will not.
- When bored, I don't need chocolate: I need stimulation.
- Eat what you like best first; you will feel satisfied more quickly.

IMAGE AND ATTITUDE

- Think and act slim to get slim.
- Awareness and attitude are as important as dietary expertise.
- I want to be the best I can be, every day of my life.
- Fat is paralysing. If I eat between meals, it's to avoid problems, boredom, and bad feelings.
- Fear of growing old and fat are blocking my energy.
- My eating habits create my reality.
- A healthy diet will help me feel good and stay healthy.
- Health is a quality – it leads to good habits.
- I am the creator of my body, and my life.
- I can go to a restaurant and be happy just to talk; I don't need to eat.
- I can't lie: my body betrays everything I eat and drink.
- I don't need dozens of outfits. I need a slim body.
- I must choose between finishing everything on my plate and feeling comfortable in my jeans.

- I will visualise my ideal weight appearing on the scales.
- I will always be conscious of my emotional problems.
- I will anticipate the effects of drinking alcohol on my body.
- I will divest from everything that saps my energy: unhealthy food, uninteresting people, cumbersome objects, mediocrity.
- I will not build up superfluous fat in my body.
- I thank my body for being in good health.
- I treat my body as I treat my best friends.
- I don't diet, I eat little. Simple!
- I am at ease with food. It enriches my life.
- My body is my temple: I treat it with respect.
- If I eat too much today, I won't be hungry tomorrow, or the day after.
- My mind thinks in pictures (food, body shape, clothes, the future).
- We lose weight when we stop fixating about the number on the scales.
- Preparing my own food is part of my health and beauty regime.
- I am nourished by quality in everything.
- My jeans are my unbiased judge.
- I must organise to get slim.
- To get slim, thoughts must be translated into action.
- What nourishes my thoughts is as important as what nourishes my body.
- If I choose what my body is asking for, I will be agreeing with myself.

BODY CARE

- I must take care of myself, to take care of others.
- I will not compromise my body with unhealthy and chemical products.
- I will note down the weight shown on the scales, no matter what it is.
- My body will become more beautiful if I exercise, eat healthily and maintain good posture.
- I will brush my body for five minutes daily.
- No fixed exercise programme – my body will decide.
- Too much rest leads to 'rustiness' and is self-destructive.

PART III

MIND

'It is absurd to ignore oneself when we want to know everything'

Platon

At an intuitive level, and despite empirical, logical assertions to the contrary, mankind has always known that diseases of the body are inseparable from those of the mind. Controlling our subconscious urges and achieving inner balance are more than a simple matter of choice, however: what's required is a complete restructuring of the way we think.

Our first duty is to take care of ourselves, make friends with ourselves, and respect ourselves. Yet cultural traditions (notably in the West and so-called 'developed' or wealthy nations) prevent us from acknowledging the positive value of self-care, equating it with individualism, and narcissism. Countering this, a long tradition of thought propounded by figures such as Socrates, Dogen, or the German theologian Meister Eckhart, recognises its importance. The same thinking underpins the teachings of Epicureanism, Stoicism, Buddhism, Hinduism and more – some of the most rigorous, austere moral codes known to East or West, but also the most universal.

Asceticism is an essential pathway to greater serenity and self-knowledge. When we strive to change, we are above all striving for liberation. Three rules guide our progress: don't ask too much of life, avoid excess, and conduct yourself with humility.

Self-care, in every culture, demands constant self-questioning. Shifting our focus to the self acknowledges the importance of concentrating on immediate, direct concerns, rather than natural catastrophes, or the evil and stupidity of the world at large. To ponder these is pointless.

We can and should take charge of ourselves. We can change and improve by practising techniques for memorising the past, by examining our own conscience, through renunciation, discipline and restraint, and by leading a rigorously structured intellectual and physical life.

The self is our constant and only goal, unchanged over time, unaffected by circumstance. We have the power to control ourselves, to correct ourselves, and to find fulfilment by so doing.

But remember, the ethic of self-care is part and parcel of our lifestyle as a whole.

Seneca urges us to protect the self, to arm it, respect it, honour it and take ownership of it; to keep it within our sight, and to organise our lives around it. Genuine self-knowledge, he maintains, is the greatest, and the only legitimate, lasting, unshakeable source of joy: 'most powerful is he who has himself in his own power'.

1

Your inner ecology

A purer spirit

ANXIETY AND STRESS

Negative, restless thoughts, suspicions and doubts pollute the mind if we allow them. We can improve our inner ecology by eliminating them and substituting a positive attitude.

Our 'inner ecology' is our inner effort of self-perfection – our 'spiritual work.' We must counter the violence and fear so often promulgated in the media, with knowledge, art, beauty, the pursuit of well-being, peace and love.

The calmer and more serene we become, the easier it will be to manage, classify and organise our storehouse of information, to use it effectively and to good purpose, to think clearly. Our true life's work is our self-preparation for a higher plane of existence.

Anxiety is a state of mind. Nothing more. Ninety per cent of the things we worry about will never happen. Major catastrophes, such as earthquakes, fires and serious illness do exist, of course, but if we allow them to dominate our thoughts, they will loom larger in our mind than in the real world. Negative emotions, anxiety and nervous depression are toxic. Feelings of rebellion, fear, jealousy, frustration, hatred and resentment are mentally and physically self-destructive. Negative thoughts obstruct the intellect and prevent the free circulation of feelings of love and happiness.

An inflexible body stems from an inflexible mind. Anxiety affects the nerve-endings in our stomach, sending messages to the brain for the secretion of excess gastric juices, which are toxic to the system. Anxiety sweeps through our nervous and glandular systems, and can cause the release of the stress hormone cortisol. Cortisol can cause fat to build up around our mid-section. This explains why some anxiety sufferers find it difficult to lose weight, even if they eat little. Anxiety affects our sleep, and leads to diabetes, wrinkles, grey hair and a dull complexion. It undermines our concentration and decision-making. It blocks energy and disrupts the metabolism. Yet anxiety is a habit of thought, nothing more! People who do not know how to combat anxiety raise their chance of an early death from heart attack or stroke by up to a fifth. People of a nervous disposition take longer to recover from illness. Nervous anxiety is a long-term malady that brings others in its wake. How can we foster a serene existence if we devote our mental energies to constant worrying?

Some doctors maintain that the neurotic fear of time itself is most harmful to body and mind alike, and that it can lead to premature ageing. But we have the power to train ourselves in practices that can bring healing, and restore us to health and happiness.

If we focus endlessly on our problems and worries, we lose sight of what we really want, and who we are. Stress dissipates us and tears us apart.

It is vitally important that we exorcise our feelings of anger, externalise them, and eliminate them from our bodies.

The basic rules for eliminating stress are as follows:

- Eat good-tasting, healthy food.
- Be physically active, oxygenate the body, swim.
- Make time for pampering treatments and pleasurable moments.
- Respect your biorhythms: digestion, the secretion of hormones, the synthesising of cholesterol, cellular regeneration. The best way to identify and learn your individual rhythms is to keep a notebook over the course of a month, writing down the times of day when you feel hungry, sleepy, or lacking in energy. Little by little, try to adjust your habits and lifestyle to take account of your personal body clock.
- Get enough sleep. Lack of sleep is a source of stress.
- Go to bed and get up at the same time each day. Sleep follows a ninety-minute cycle. If you miss the onset of one cycle, you must wait for the next.
- Enjoy your food, and eat in calm, convivial surroundings. Avoid noisy restaurants, frozen food, industrial 'ready meals'.
- Eat simply prepared dishes, fresh vegetables, fish, quality vegetable oils, seasonal fruits.
- Remember that a meal enjoyed in quiet surroundings will impact the metabolism differently from a meal taken in

'unfavourable' conditions. Your digestion will be disrupted, slowing your metabolism.

- Take a moment for yourself at lunchtime. Say 'no' to forced invitations, and to fatty or sugary foods.
- Allow yourself a little fine-quality, very dark chocolate each day, as a source of magnesium. It will enhance your sleep, too.
- Remember that excess alcohol consumption disrupts sleep, and diminishes its restorative power.
- Never eat too much or too little (except when fasting). Often, hunger is in the mind, not the stomach.
- Eat a full breakfast. Ideally, this will be your main daily meal, and comprise hearty, savoury dishes. Breakfast is literally, as the name implies, the breaking of a fast.
- Take physical exercise. Sport is the best anti-stress activity. It should be regulated, taken in appropriate measure, and as part of a balanced lifestyle. Better to take ten minutes of daily exercise than an hour once a week.
- Walk in the countryside or a park. Walking clarifies the thoughts and helps put problems in perspective. Remember to breathe the negative ions beside a stretch of water.
- Yawn, laugh, don't take things too seriously.

Stress will gnaw at your system if you let it. Practise building a wall of serenity against it.

WE ARE WHAT WE THINK

Our joys and sufferings are writ large and easily read in our face and expression – in our skin tone and complexion, our scars, our 'character lines'.

A life lived without cultivating an awareness of who we truly are leads to self-deterioration and destruction. Our lives are what we make of them, in our own minds. Energy waves are essential to our make-up, and we have the power to alter the processes by which they work, to find meaning in our everyday lives, and to open the doors wide to the possibilities within us.

This can only occur, however, when we become properly aware of our actions and thoughts. Our subconscious works 24/7, storing our thoughts away. Each thought is a cause; the mindset that results is its effect. We must take charge of our thoughts, if they are to shape only the most favourable outcomes.

Our inner world shapes our outer world. Learn to select your thoughts. Choose to be pleasant, cheerful, warm and loving – the world will return your choice in kind.

Concentrate your mind on the conviction that only good things will come, and be careful to 'watch' your thoughts, so that you may direct them to things that are right, excellent and reasonable.

Your inner thoughts are reflected in every aspect of your appearance and conduct. Think of your mind as a garden. You can choose the seeds you sow. Your subconscious is a tapestry of the ideas you sow all day long. You will harvest the results in vitality, health, friends, social status and a sound financial situation. It is vitally important, then, to pay close attention to your thoughts. Energy flows from your thoughts: they are the origin of your attitude to life.

You are responsible for your own existence. The world you create around you is its reflection.

Health is a question of attitude. Living well means never letting go of the very best of yourself, deep down inside. The way you think and express yourself conditions your physical conduct, your posture, and your well-being (or lack of it). You will only grow strong if you know how to lead a peaceful, balanced existence.

CLEARING YOUR MIND

The followers of Wu Wei believed that the best phase of existence begins when we have cleared our minds of useless thoughts.

We live in a psychological prison of our own making, chained by our beliefs, opinions and education, and by external, environmental influences.

If our minds are cluttered and congested, we cannot function normally. We will overreact, become distracted by non-essentials, and be unable to concentrate.

As we grow older, our minds become more cluttered, like an attic full of useless, forgotten things. We never stop thinking, consciously or otherwise. How do we spend our time? What are our ambitions? Are we fighting for things that truly matter?

As with material possessions, clearing or tidying our mind means getting rid of anything that is irrelevant (or no longer contributes) to our specific, immediate needs. In this way, we make room for things of greater importance. Each thought makes its mark on the brain, reinforcing or weakening our immune system.

Just as an absence of objects makes for a simpler life, so

'gettings thing off our mind' makes room for new ideas. Practise 'rubbing out' or removing specific ideas: the actions they engender will be eradicated too.

Make a list of the ideas or thoughts that surface most often in your mind, playing on a loop all day long, over and over: thoughts to which you have become so accustomed, it no longer occurs to you to chase them away.

Take time over your list, draw it up carefully, and in detail. If you find certain items difficult or tiresome, set them aside and find a moment to focus on their content. Once the list is firmly established, try to chase each thought out of your mind. Take them one by one, patiently, over the course of a day. Push them away gently but firmly, each time they recur. This practice, like every other, will bear fruit: the day will come when you are surprised to find new thoughts taking their place.

ARE YOU ASKING YOURSELF THE RIGHT QUESTIONS?

Each question should be specific and unambiguous, for its potential answer to be heard. Each should be formulated as simply as possible. We have a choice in everything we do. There are reasons why we focus on certain choices, and not on others. Some people are drawn to a beautiful object, others notice interesting people in the crowd around it, or the trash containers placed (almost) out of sight nearby – life's faults and imperfections. Most of the time, these choices are unconscious, but we can make better use of our conscious mind, and use it as a tool to inform our choices. If we find ourselves noticing only negative things, we can take corrective action and seek out other, more positive things.

In one sense, life is a continuous, creative act. We can instruct our subconscious to select only those things that are most pertinent to our future.

NEGATIVITY

Anxiety and regrets have no place in a mind suffused with the simple truth that there are no highs without lows. Life is seldom as dark as it might seem when we are sunk in the trough between two peaks. If we continue to act as we have always done, we will be what we have always been. Our limitations are wholly self-imposed. True self-esteem comes when we master our self-image as the pathway to liberation. We can practise developing our patience, like a muscle that grows stronger the more it is exercised.

The mind is a creative organ. Life forgives us if we cut a finger: new cells are formed, healing the cut. The same is true of our thoughts.

Each time you feel the onset of anxiety, each time you feel lost, alone, depressed, full of bitterness, negativity or anger, take up an interesting book, put on a different outfit and do whatever you can to make your surroundings brighter and more cheerful: buy flowers, put on music, light incense, or a scented candle. You might make time for some yoga, a few gym exercises, to write in your diary, take a bath or go out for a walk. The important thing is to stop the flow of negative thoughts until new energy replaces what was there before.

TRANSCEND YOUR PROBLEMS

'Faced with a problem, there is nothing to do.'

Dr Charles Barker

Don't tackle or 'treat' your problems: rise above them. Focusing on a problem keeps it alive and prevents you from moving on. Negative thoughts do not need to be analysed, dissected, studied – if we do, they spread. Refuse to poison your life with old habits, old grudges, unforgiven wounds. Consign the detritus of the past to the waste-paper basket. Keep only good memories.

Life begins anew each day. You are alive today, here and now. Stop believing the person you were yesterday is the person you have to be today. Everyone has limitless potential, and the possibility to change if we truly want to. What prevents us from tapping that potential (it's a vicious circle) is our psychological attachment to the past. The energy and drive we have right now are all we need.

Tackle difficult situations by focusing on simple details. Whatever we focus on grows in importance. The more we focus on things we don't want to think about, the more power they will have over us. Instead of thinking actively about a problem, forget it. The simple fact of recognising the true nature of what's at stake, and the right questions to ask, is enough. Let the question rest, and settle, like still water. Soon, something magical will take place in your subconscious. When we obsess about a problem, or something that irritates us, we forget the wonders and possibilities of life. We see only what is lacking, the injustice, the causes of our unhappiness, our frustrations, our sorrow. But the hard times in life offer an opportunity to step back and reconsider. At such times, ask yourself: 'What is more important? Why did I do that?'

We know there exists a force we can access at any moment in our lives: we just need to ask our psyche to 'plug in' to the current. The greater our awareness, the better we are able to tackle our problems. If we focus endlessly on the obstacles, problems and difficulties before us, our subconscious will act accordingly and block the doors of happiness. Whatever happens teaches us something.

NEGATIVITY HURTS

We do ourselves as much harm by negative thinking and behaviour as we do by an unhealthy diet, smoking or lack of sleep. Our frustrations are the result of unfulfilled desires, anxiety is the result of uncertainty, and negativity is the result of low energy and self-esteem.

Healing the psyche involves taking action to bring things that were unconscious to the surface of our conscious minds. First, identify the source of your negative moods, then ask what it is you really want.

Draw up a list of your heart's desires. Don't focus on whether or not they are achievable, or how. Properly directed thoughts can generate energy waves, to be harnessed as inspiration. In the same way, with regular practice, we can learn how to chase out negative thoughts. We can all learn to combat negative thoughts, just as we learn to ride a bicycle, swim, or drive. Once learned, these skills become automatic.

With practice, a mindset of serenity can be achieved in less than a month. Often, when we are ill, we heal faster if we drive out negative thoughts.

All thoughts dwindle into nothingness eventually. Be aware of the power of your thoughts. Is it your feelings that are negative, or your life? Recognise the tremendous power of your subconscious mind. It is capable of bringing you happiness, health, liberation – everything you deserve.

Don't focus on the past. Concentrate instead on what you can do here and now. Each morning, for example, try asking yourself what sort of day you would like to have. Try to bring to mind everything that is good and pleasant in your life: a pessimist will quickly realise the extent of his negativity. As his thinking becomes more constructive, he will be more and more motivated to reach for things that will elevate his outlook.

Before going to sleep, practise reviewing the enjoyable moments of your day: a walk, a good meal, a meeting with a friend. These are your treasures. Note them down quickly in your diary. Later, they will remind you of the great sum of happiness your life has brought you. Make a prayer, and ask your subconscious to answer it, review your thoughts and tell yourself that you will sleep soundly. Dreams can begin before going to sleep.

Self-control: all in the mind

STEP OUTSIDE YOURSELF

Imagine you have the magical power to step outside your own body and sit down next to yourself. Look at yourself. What is this person like? What do they look like? Do you like them? Do you like yourself? Can you help this person, can you advise them?

Practise self-detachment. Don't cling to your thoughts or ideas. When we decide to put an end to something, even a consuming passion, the spectacle of our own success is our greatest reward, together with the realisation that the renunciation has not prevented you from living your life. You will experience a great sense of relief, a feeling of lightness. You will be able to tell yourself: 'I've done it, I'm rid of it!'

When you have truly 'cleared your mind', when you find yourself floating free, when your actions are dictated by nothing but the here and now, when objectivity and subjectivity are one and the same, you will have attained the highest state of detachment. Your ultimate goal is to free yourself from whatever is tying you down. Techniques exist to help you take control of your life, your stress levels, the waves of confusion that can overwhelm us physically and undermine our morale.

UPHOLD YOUR PRINCIPLES

'Principles are deep, fundamental truths ... they are tightly
woven threads running with exactness, consistency, beauty,
and strength throughout the fabric of life.'

Stephen Covey, *The Seven Habits of Highly Effective People*

We don't always know what we want: we want to lose weight, but we also want to eat that slice of cake.

And so we need principles. Applying principles can become a habit, an automatic reflex, if we make the effort to apply them consistently over a period of time.

We don't always know how to choose: to help our mind dictate our behaviour, we need the backing of specific principles. So many are so simple, yet we fail to apply them: living a balanced lifestyle, showing good sense and respect for the environment. Our ambitions and principles are the pillars of our existence. Without them, we lack direction and feel lost.

KNOW HOW TO DECIDE

Making good, swift decisions is an art, and a quality – it prevents us from fretting more than we need. Once a decision has been taken, and the necessary action accomplished, we may consider the problem solved, and strive to put it out of our minds. Try to take more of your own decisions. Strength of character is a vital force, and essential when it comes to making choices and taking decisions. Security, wisdom and strength are interdependent. Try to rediscover the inventive outlook you had as a child.

Making good choices is one of our most creative gifts. Each minute of our lives forces us to make choices, and presents innumerable possibilities. But once we have made space for the new and the unknown, we can open the door to a more profound existence, while we wait for life's empty, hollow moments to rise to the surface and vanish like bubbles. Be attentive to the things you desire. This is the only way to discover your passions. A life filled with joy is filled with abundance, too.

Mindfulness and meditation

DEVELOP YOUR CONCENTRATION: MEDITATE

*'Only let the troubled waters be calm, and the sun and moon
will be reflected on the surface of your being.'*

Rumi (thirteenth-century Sufi poet)

Create empty space around yourself. Don't allow yourself to be distracted by noise, faces, your nearest and dearest. Create empty space in order to concentrate on a single subject, or rather on the relationship between yourself and it. You are aiming to neutralise your thoughts, your desires and your imagination.

Begin by aiming for a state of 'non-thinking'. At first, ideas will recur: push them gently away. Erase them again and again, even for only thirty seconds. You will see it can be done. This is the first step. Yogis can remain in this state for an entire day. If you practise emptying your mind of thoughts, regularly and diligently, they will float to the surface, but their presence will be felt less and less, and they will be more easily rejected. Training yourself to meditate or control your mind is like training a muscle in the body. Patience and perseverance will produce results.

When a person meditates, they sink into a state of repose twice as deep as that of sleep. The body consumes more oxygen, the heartbeat rises, and the mind is alert. It takes ten minutes to reach this state in meditation, but six hours when asleep.

During meditation, all ambivalence, all dependence on others, all attachments, disappear completely. We feel a tremendous sense of freedom: this is the quickest and simplest path to happiness. Allow things to take their course, as if you weren't involved. After a time, you will feel utterly detached. Meditation can be practised anywhere, even while waiting for a bus or doing the dishes. Golf is excellent for meditation, relaxation and peace of mind. A golfer once said that, at the end of a round, he felt as much at peace with himself as a Buddhist monk on the summit of a mountain. What matters is to take a moment to pay attention to your inner self. This is a source of strength found nowhere else. Meditation is not vacuous. It does not induce a state of torpor – it is a stringent mental discipline, a process by which we sharpen our conscious-ness and our powers of concentration, both of which are extremely useful in everyday life.

'But I don't have time,' as someone once said . . .

The verb 'to meditate' (*meditari* in Latin) means to allow oneself to be lead towards the centre. Things that have become fixed will dominate and block the mind. Take time, quite simply, to 'be'; allow your mind to recharge in silence. From time to time, set your own image aside and revisit the sensation of being someone completely new.

There are times when we need to learn how to do nothing. Meditation helps us understand how our psyche functions. Before practising it, people are often unaware of just how many scattered ideas pass through their mind in the space of a second. These fleeting thoughts complicate our lives.

Meditation is nourishment for the psyche. It enables us to achieve self-renewal and to reaffirm the essential things in life. Running on a beach, sitting in a wood, listening to music – activities such as these take time. We can meditate – in other words, keep our mind active and mobile – when walking, sitting, standing or lying down.

The body must be silenced for meditation by adopting specific postures (yoga offers a number of options, including the lotus position, and *shavasana* – lying on your back on the floor, in a state of total relaxation, eyes closed). Slow your breathing as far as possible. Silence your thoughts. Refuse anything that will bring you out of your state of non-thinking.

The Zen Buddhist master Deshimaru said that thoughts should be allowed to float like clouds in the sky; he advised his followers to 'be life' rather than thinking about it. Meditation enhances blood circulation and memory. It obliges us to seek inner silence and to economise our words, focusing instead on internal, organic sounds, our heartbeat and breathing.

Meditate to find 'ground zero' in your own mental and muscular activity. Experience the sense of heat and weight suffusing your body. Express what you are feeling by talking to yourself: 'I feel heat flowing into my body . . .' Anchor each new sensation in words, a simple statement. Later, simply repeat the phrase to experience the sensation.

QUIET MORNINGS

'I decided to ... have no special attitude of mind whatsoever ...
it seemed that I threw myself away as well, for quite suddenly
the weight of my own body disappeared. I felt that I owned
nothing, not even a self, and that nothing owned me. The
whole world became as transparent and unobstructed as my
own mind.'

Alan Watts, *Zen Buddhism*

Meditate in the morning, when the air is fresh and free of artificial vibrations. The more you concentrate on the details of your environment, the more immediate your perceptions will be. Observe your emotions as external phenomena that cannot touch you. In this way, you will learn not to be a slave to your regrets, your impatience, your anxiety, to confused thinking of every kind. You will even succeed in forgetting the present, and discover that you enjoy the experience! When you achieve non-thinking, you will have reached your goal. Things will become simpler. Your responsibilities and obligations will drift away. Accept the ideas floating to the surface, but do not attribute any significance to them. If you succeed in non-thinking, you will experience intense repose. In sleep, we rest but we also dream, hence we do not experience the complete mental repose that can be achieved in meditation.

Make time, and create a suitable space in a small, secluded corner of your home. Install a large, comfortable cushion of pure wool or silk, and a small altar (a plank of wood at eye level is all you need) on which to place a candle, a flower and an incense stick. Buddhist monks or nuns use the stick to time the session, which will last around twenty minutes. Allow the fragrance and silence to envelop you, be aware of the softness of your cushion, breathe deeply two or three times, to exhale your negative thoughts, and take twenty minutes simply to sit. Unless you have practised it and are very supple, the lotus position is uncomfortable, so don't be tempted to try it: you cannot silence your body if it is causing you pain. For this reason, exercises to enhance your suppleness are an indispensable preparation for meditation, too. The correct posture is all-important, for many reasons, but chiefly as an aid to concentration. Other positions (seated in an armchair or lying stretched out on the floor) will not allow you to reach a true state of perfect, non-thinking fulfilment.

SILENCE IS GOLDEN

'Stop talking and thinking: there will be nothing you cannot understand.'

Buddhist proverb

Silence allows us to be attentive to everything, to observe the 'mental flotsam' passing endlessly through our minds. Learning not to respond continually to these stimuli requires an open mind, time and patience. In the media and online, avoid programmes and articles or reports that contribute nothing to your existence and rob you of precious time, mental space, and silence. Their effect is soporific, lulling us into a state of mind-numbing passivity. They are 'chewing gum for the eyes'. Silence enables you to stretch out in its own void. It is a receptive space. Let it be your guide.

LA GOUTTE INCANDESCENTE

*'Science is the tool of the Western mind and with it more
doors can be opened than with bare hands. It is part
and parcel of our knowledge and obscures our insight only
when it holds that the understanding given by it is the
only kind there is. The East has taught us another, wider,
more profound, and higher understanding, that is,
understanding through life.'*

Carl Jung, commentary on *The Secret of the Golden Flower*

ONE THOUGHT AT A TIME

*'To sit and meditate for hours, eating when our body asks us
and live in a simple hut, what luxury!'*

Urabe Kenko, *Essays in Idleness*

Visualise a phrase. The goal of meditation is attained when even the idea of 'non-thinking' has floated away. In meditation, even physical sensations disappear, meaning that their specific energy has been confiscated and repurposed to enhance our clarity of consciousness. We all need to spend time alone, in contemplation, centring ourselves on a single thought, reading, studying or working. Even arranging flowers in a vase in the morning can become a meditative exercise. Your day will be transformed! Many people live their lives in the grip of passions, which are a form of passivity in themselves, a way to forget their own selves. But a person who stays sitting in meditation, contemplating their own self, is far more connected to the world. Meditation is the highest form of activity granted to man, in his quest for liberation and independence. Taoists believe that matter is essentially spiritual, and that beauty and intelligence are there, right in front of us. If we cannot see them, our own senses are at fault.

A person can attain this intuitive knowledge through rest, non-attachment and contemplation. A person can free themselves from time, space, everyday life, desires, received wisdom, and ultimately their own self.

2

Other people

Simplify your contacts

CHOOSE OUR RELATIONSHIPS, BE TOLERANT

'Only the perfect man can live among his peers without accepting their prejudices. He adapts to them without losing his personality. He learns nothing from them and recognises their aspirations without making them his own.'

Zhuang Zhou

Break off sterile relationships. End relationships that give you no support. In love, never be the slave of the person you desire. Avoid people of little intelligence. Better not to spend time with them, than to criticise them. But do not confuse intelligence and intellectual aptitude: there are many forms of intelligence – emotional intelligence, intelligent good sense. Some people have neither.

People are separated more by their social milieu, money, religious beliefs and aspirations than by anything else, including race or culture. Intolerant, uncomprehending people can prevent us from growing and moving forward. Slowly but surely diminish their importance in your life. And don't waste another minute thinking about people you don't like.

Don't try to adapt to uncomfortable situations, and don't demand excessive openness and sincerity from others. You don't have to bare your soul to someone to be close to them. Leave the world and its rules outside – the world that insists we take other people's needs into consideration, and forces us to hide behind a plethora of masks. We will be much happier if we learn to live with our own and others' imperfections.

Out and about

LEARN TO SAY NO

'The only man who is really free is the one who can turn down an invitation to dinner without giving an excuse.'

Jules Renard

In Western society, it is more acceptable to be polite and hypocritical than to be direct and honest. If you find it difficult to say 'no', remember that you say 'no' to someone else in order to say 'yes' to yourself. If you refuse an invitation to a party with friends, the person who invited you is unlikely to be massively offended. If, however, you find it impossible to just say 'no', try saying: 'OK, I'm free on Friday, but only until 8.00 p.m.' A simple explanation, with as few details as possible, is the best way to refuse. Practise saying: 'I'm so sorry, I really don't have time at the moment, but I'll call you as soon as my schedule allows.' Don't feel you must change your plans to accommodate those of other people. Don't worry about what they will think or say about you as a result. You will feel liberated. When you compromise your dreams or values for another person, you lose a little of yourself and your strength. The more you compromise your authentic nature, the weaker and more vulnerable you will feel. Offload anything that does not enrich your life; cut the bonds that tie you to beliefs, values and obligations which may have been genuine at one time in your life, but which have no place in your identity now. Don't be the person everyone expects you to be – be the person *you* want to be. Know precisely and firmly the things you want and do not want in your life. Be independent. Have the courage to say 'no' with a smile, and with no excuses. No one and nothing has the slightest power over you: we are all in sole control of our own thoughts. Manage your thoughts to achieve a harmonious, balanced mindset: you'll soon find this applies to your life as a whole.

GIVE LESS, RECEIVE MORE

Giving and receiving . . . Simplify your relationships with others and rediscover a more natural way to behave. Don't feel embarrassed to 'receive' from others. When you know, at the bottom of your heart, that you are not taking advantage of another person's generosity, you can accept what they are offering with simple gratitude.

Don't be 'generous to a fault'. Too often, we give to others in order to feel better and experience pleasure ourselves. Even if we expect nothing back in return, we feel piqued if the recipient doesn't thank us for our gift, or reacts to it in a way that is different from how we might have reacted ourselves.

Above all, avoid financial transactions with your friends if you don't want to cloud your friendship. Don't talk about your problems. Offering too much 'free advice' is a mistake too: things that are given for free have no value. If you help others too much, they won't learn how to cope on their own. The only truly valuable gift is a sense of self-control and discipline, a calm presence, and a listening, benevolent ear. Assure the other person that they can rely on you, give them the gift of your strong presence and resilience. For yourself, know the calm of mind that comes with the realisation that you can obtain whatever you need, for yourself. We are too often tempted to excessive generosity. Most of the time, we give in the hope of securing love or friendship, fearing that people will not simply appreciate us for what we are.

LEARN TO LISTEN

'We have two ears and one mouth so that we can listen twice as much as we speak.'

Chinese proverb

A talkative person is like an empty vase. Listening while keeping perfectly still, like a statue, full of grace and solemnity, was an essential part of education in antiquity. This attentive posture was a badge of a person's morality. Anyone who had mastered it radiated peace and tranquillity.

Silence reveals something profound, wonderful and sobering in the character of a person who knows how to listen. Practise your own strict economy of non-essential words and gestures in the presence of others. Discover for yourself the intimate benefits of the energy you save, and your enhanced impact on others.

WATCH YOUR WORDS

'The language we use to refer to ourselves is of tremendous
importance ... The mind-body system ... organises itself
around verbal experiences, and the wounds delivered in
words can create far more permanent effects than physical
trauma, for we literally create ourselves out of words. ...
Words are more than symbols, they are triggers of biological
information.'

Deepak Chopra, *Ageless Body, Timeless Mind*

A golden rule: if you have nothing good or kind to say, say nothing. Do as you would be done by: treat others with justice, kindness and respect.

Things assume the importance we give them. Talk about misery and unhappiness, and you'll have more of it in your life. Say something funny, and you'll have more laughter.

Take a deep breath before speaking. You will be shown more attention and respect. Let others speak freely. Let them finish what they have to say.

When you do something good, say nothing about it to others: the effect is magical – rather than diluting your satisfaction, you will be keeping it all for yourself.

Talking too much drains our energy and deprives our words of weight. If we talk too much, we feel heavy-handed and guilty for importuning others. People often talk for their own satisfaction, or so that others may benefit from their experience. They talk about themselves far too often. Stop talking about your mishaps and ills. You will exhaust yourself, and the people to whom you are talking.

The more we speak, the more distanced we become from others and ourselves.

Avoid metaphysical and religious discussions. These are the best way to make enemies. Remember, too, that there are times to talk about more profound subjects, and others when it is advisable to keep things on the surface. Learn to choose these moments.

DON'T BE CRITICAL

Critical comments say nothing about others, but a great deal about yourself: you will be known as a critical person. When you criticise someone, you create an awkward situation, and you devalue yourself. Judging others takes energy, and puts you in a situation best avoided. Above all, criticising others becomes a habit. Learn never to speak ill of anyone, whatever you might think about them. Soon, this new habit will be second nature. Criticising someone may bring relief of a kind, but other subjects of conversation are possible. Be loyal to absent friends and acquaintances. Defend them. You will earn the trust of the people you're with. Beware of duplicity. Treat everyone according to the same principles. Don't focus on other people's faults, but take a close look at your own instead. Focus your mind on more pleasant things than other people's ills and misfortunes: the mysteries of nature, true stories, a stay in the country – a source of pleasure for the scenery, the peace and quiet, and the comfort it procures. Substitute these things for curiosity over others' affairs.

No one can live in place of others.

DON'T REMONSTRATE

'What you do speaks so loudly I cannot hear what you say.'

Ralph Waldo Emerson

Self-control is essential for good relationships with others. Avoid parading your knowledge and expertise or posing as a fount of philosophical wisdom. To empty your mind is to become rich. We often talk louder than we realise. We try to expound on ideas we admire. We play the roles of people we would like to become, but these are false by definition. Don't just recite empty life maxims and affirmations. Make sure you put them into action and actively show their effects. Don't tell others how to eat, but conduct yourself during a meal as you know you should. Don't brag about the things you do.

Altruism and solitude

TAKE CARE OF YOURSELF, TO CARE BETTER FOR OTHERS

'Self-love ... is not so vile a sin as self-neglecting.'

Shakespeare

Many people live in a kind of emotional fog; they perform empty gestures, lack confidence, feel unworthy of love, and find solace in alcohol, smoking, work, or watching TV.

If you take care of yourself, you will not only be kinder to others, you will feel happier too. Don't mistreat yourself. Learn self-esteem. Treat yourself with love, and you will treat others the same. Discover the things that give you pleasure and joy, and act accordingly. Smile and laugh as often as possible. Holding yourself in proper esteem is an effective way to beat stress. Guilt is a poison that gnaws us from within.

FORGIVENESS IS GOOD FOR YOU

Forgiveness doesn't mean accepting whatever's happened. It means that you refuse to allow adversity to poison your life. Forgive for your own good, and for no other reason. But we can only forgive when we are no longer hurting. No one can hurt us unless we allow them to do so. Hurt only occurs when we interpret the facts of what has occurred in our own minds. If we are content merely to position ourselves as a witness to the facts, we will not suffer. We will be able to look beyond subjective interpretations.

EXPECT NOTHING OF OTHERS

You and you alone are responsible for your own actions. You don't have to feel guilty on behalf of anyone else. But don't count on others in order to be happy. Are you truly so wonderful that the whole world demands your presence? On the other hand, do you want people to feel sorry for you? If you don't enjoy your own company, it's unlikely others will appreciate it either. People who demand happiness from others feel unable to deliver it for themselves. People who expect nothing, regret nothing and have nothing to lose are to be admired. They are not influenced by people or things, and know how to find infinite resources within themselves.

DON'T TRY TO CHANGE OTHER PEOPLE

Whatever you do, don't try to change other people. This will only complicate your life, drain your energy, and leave you feeling helpless and frustrated. Stop explaining. Be happy to let others ask you the secret of your serene happiness. The only way to influence others is by example: behave in such a way that they will seek to emulate your lifestyle, your attitudes, your ideas. Everyone seeks to emulate people who radiate happiness. Helping others means encouraging them to think. The distinguished historian Arnold Toynbee once said that the future of humanity depends on the degree to which each of us is capable of retreating into ourselves and finding our own depths, so that we may draw on the best of ourselves to help others.

Resist the pathological need to be always right. You don't need to be everyone's planner or timekeeper. Intervene only when you feel it necessary; the rest of the time, do nothing. Say nothing. You will inspire more respect as a result. If you seek to defend your position, you will simply be wasting your energy.

BE YOURSELF

'I don't like competitions; the only person I measure myself against is me. There are no winners, there are only differences.'

An athlete's words

Maintaining your integrity requires detachment. You have no need to aspire to be like others, or to be different from them. A person with few attachments feels free. The best way to better humanity is to better yourself.

WHAT WE CAN GIVE OTHERS

Our greatest gift to other people is to behave in such a way that they aspire to become simpler and more spontaneous themselves, to think less about themselves, and to focus only on a few core desires. In an ideal society, where no one seeks to accumulate wealth and riches, there are no thieves. The richer our inner life, the greater our self-esteem, and the more we have to give.

Offering practical help to others is a good thing, but helping them to think for themselves is far more important. If we can help others to detach from their desires, even for an hour, we prove to them that with determination and practice, they can continue in the same way for the rest of their lives. This is the greatest help we can give anyone. By giving other people the example of our own conduct and lifestyle, by demonstrating our enjoyment of life regardless of our personal circumstances, we can encourage them to focus only on simple, spontaneous things. We can prove that a person's happiness is far greater when they don't think too much about themselves but focus on only a few core desires. We are impoverished by our belief that happiness comes with material possessions. Impoverished when we allow ourselves to be influenced by advertising. Impoverished when we allow ourselves to be caught up in the relentless machinery of competitiveness. Impoverished when we cannot free ourselves to live simpler lives. Impoverished when we attach labels to everything, even to generosity itself.

Poverty is not a lack of money. It is a lack of human, spiritual and intellectual qualities. Helping others means not parading your wealth, but living simply and respecting your fellow humans without judging them. It also means not making them feel jealous, bitter, or envious.

CULTIVATE THE ART OF LIVING ALONE

'My greatest pleasure is napping and contemplating the
seasons. The whole world is only the awareness we have of it.
If the heart is at peace, even the most valuable treasure is
worth nothing. I like my poor home. I feel sorry for all these
slaves of the material world. The only way to appreciate
solitude is to live it.'

Kamo no Chomei, *Notes de ma cabane*

'Alone' derives from the phrase 'all one'. Savour your moments of solitude. Being alone is not a choice, it is our original condition. We are all alone, deep down inside. Solitude can be difficult for a person who is unused to it but, over time, it becomes a precious commodity. Physical solitude is not to be feared, but spiritual solitude is. If we feel alone in our heart, how can we truly experience contact with others, when we are in their company? Solitude helps us to recover our energies. The loneliness of the true 'solitary' is superficial. The solitary's mind is peopled with beings and ideas, it is a secret cavern where a thousand conversations take place.

Appreciate solitude. Consider it a privilege, not an ordeal. It is a gift from heaven, and the essential condition for self-advancement, the consideration of serious topics, or effective work. Moments of solitude enable us to plant seeds that will grow and flourish in unknown, still-undiscovered phases of life. Learn to appreciate your own company before it is forced upon you. There is a strong chance that each of us will spend several years of our lives alone. We may as well be prepared, and well prepared at that. Living alone is an art to be learned and cultivated. There are so many things we can accomplish in silence and solitude! Meditating, reading, dreaming, imagining, creating, taking care of ourselves.

Learn to be happy for yourself alone: cook food, dig your garden, go foraging, beautify your body, your home, your thoughts. Try spending a night in a small hotel from time to time: take a novel, read it on a sunny café terrace, enjoy a picnic beside a stretch of water. You will appreciate the presence of others all the more, and give them more than you ever have before. Solitude enriches our life!

3

Polish yourself like a pebble

Be ready to change

HAVE FAITH IN YOURSELF

'We are such stuff as dreams are made on.'

Shakespeare

We have far richer resources at our disposal than we could ever imagine.

Have faith in yourself and you will discover that everything (or almost everything) is possible. If you live by your dreams and your aspirations, you will achieve your heart's desire. If you redouble your efforts to achieve a specific goal, you will see surprising results. Choose to believe that beneficial things will come to you.

'Successful' people (great job, beautiful family . . .) never doubt their own ability to obtain the things they aspire to. Success is rooted in the mind, and finds expression in the material world, never the other way around. To obtain prosperity, you must first create it in your own mind. Our thoughts have extraordinary power. We all share this advantage, and we should all use it. It is within our power to think for ourselves. Provided we keep an open mind and are receptive, we can make use of all the intelligence lying untapped in the spheres of our subconscious mind.

Don't doubt the success of your projects. To find a new way forward, first rid yourself of old habits of thought. Try not to doubt yourself. Doubt is a waste of energy that will block the successful completion of any project.

Tell yourself you are not a creative person, and you will never become one. You are the person blocking your own creativity (though in the case of children, parents sometimes stand in their way, and in the case of couples, one partner may hinder the other). Never forget that you are a person of passion, talent, intelligence, wisdom, creativity and depth. Choose to obtain the things you dream of, or your fears will be realised instead. We create and see the things we expect to see. If you approach a situation with feelings of prejudice and negativity, you will suffer their negative outcomes. We create our own realities. Fear causes us to cling inflexibly to our old habits. If we persuade ourselves that only one course of action is available, we become tense and strained. Other possibilities are always available; we just have to seek them out. What happens to us is not important, it's how we deal with it that matters. Stop obsessing about things you don't want to happen. Know in your heart of hearts that you will succeed, rather than merely hoping you might. Identify the problem clearly. Ask your subconscious to find a solution and relax in the certainty that everything will turn out for the best. If you try hard to concentrate, your scheme will fail. Feeling successful generates success. Remain as open as possible to every eventuality. Believe. Your own words have the power to cleanse your spirit of false ideas, and to instil right ideas in their place. Allow one single thought to float to the surface of your consciousness: the belief that whatever happens is for the best. Be sure to fill your mind with things that are pleasant, true and 'right'. By changing the way you think, you will alter your destiny. The things you believe in won't produce results, but the sincerity of your belief will.

VISUALISE THE PERSON YOU WANT TO BE

Once the subconscious has accepted an idea, it sets about putting it into practice. If you plan to write a book, make a discovery or implement a new lifestyle, develop the idea in your head first, down to the last detail, and apply yourself to believing the change is a reality here and now. A thought is a form of reality in itself. Your subconscious has already accepted it as such. We've all experienced receiving unexpected good news, a telephone call that has got us out of an awkward situation, a windfall when it was most needed. We tend to think of such moments as pure coincidences, but they may not be the product of chance after all. Our body is the direct expression of our intentions up to this point. If we imagine an experience with sufficient intensity, a whole range of involuntary reactions will be set in motion, conforming precisely to what we have 'foreseen' in our mind's eye.

Sit down, relax and try to think of nothing at all. Darken your surroundings, to help you forget the outside world. Try to move as little as possible, this will help achieve calmness of mind and enhance your receptivity to new suggestions. Visualise how you would like something to unfold; picture the scenario with as much detail and precision as possible. Reject all fears, all concerns, destructive thoughts of any kind. New ideas will emerge, and you will 'awaken' feeling rested, calm and serene.

DISTIL YOURSELF TO YOUR PUREST ESSENCE

'Everyone, when they are young, knows what their destiny is. At that point in their lives, everything is clear, everything is possible. They are not afraid to dream and to yearn for everything they would like to happen to them in their lives.'

Paulo Coelho, *The Alchemist*, tr. Alan R. Clarke

No part of our being remains unchanged over the course of our lives. Showing readiness to accept change proves that we are not set in our ways, that we are still young at heart. When we cease to accept change, we die.

We create our own reality at every moment in our lives, through our ideas and conduct. We need to realise the price we pay for negative thinking. Spiritual progress implies change, relinquishing one thing for another – habits, points of view, expectations or demands. Don't feel self-pity. Correct yourself instead. Find the best in any situation, and stop talking about your woes to others. At the same time, try to confront issues head-on. Living with constant, unfocused anxiety can become a habit, and ultimately a chronic condition. When this happens, we stop thinking about ways to rid ourselves of anxiety, or how life might be different if we accepted change. The key to change is the conviction that deep down inside, there is an immutable 'me'. A 'me' that has unique value. This 'me' is our magnetic pole: it remains fixed, while all around it can change without fear or difficulty.

Viktor Frankl, the celebrated Viennese psychotherapist and Holocaust survivor, developed a complete therapeutic and philosophical system known as logotherapy during his incarceration under the Nazis. He taught his fellow inmates that many so-called mental or psychological illnesses are symptoms of a deep sense of existential emptiness, a failure to discover meaning in life. Frankl taught that each person needs to discover their mission in life, a unique mission that they and they alone can fulfil, whether in the arts, or as labourers, parents, children or spouses.

The accumulated strata of past ideas should be cleared away and replaced with new ideas.

BECOME YOUR OWN BEST FRIEND

Shine by your own light, not the lights trained on you by others. Often, people we admire and look up to have identified which aspects of their past behaviour were harmful to themselves, corrected those mistakes and become their own best friends. Be your own best friend, too. You are all you need. Treat yourself just as you treat your family, clients and friends.

Buddha left all his possessions behind. We are all condemned, sooner or later, to leave behind the 'things' of life. What will remain? We should find fulfilment in ourselves, but society does its utmost to ensure we are steered away from our own true identity. We lie to ourselves constantly. We do not trust to life, nor to our own resources. If we do not move forward, if we succumb to spiritual lethargy, if we grant others the power to control our lives, we run the risk of returning into the past. Loving yourself is the way to happiness. Accept yourself, and you will be freed from anxious thoughts about what others think of you. Respect your dreams, follow your desires.

THE DIAMOND INSIDE

We are all, in our different ways, like rough diamonds. The more we polish and shape ourselves, the more we sparkle and the more others are attracted to what they see. Apply yourself to the pursuit of perfection: it is the key to long life. Eat little and well, get to bed early, take exercise, never stop learning, meet people, make the most of new ideas and find as much joy as you can in each new day.

Know how to dress simply, choose trustworthy friends who deserve your friendship, read enriching books, create a quality environment and show good sense whenever and wherever you can.

Take your own life decisions. Plan your journeys, your time, design your own clothes, or your entire wardrobe. Use your talents and abilities, your imagination, your consciousness. Harness yourself to the future, not the past. Become your own creator. We can inhabit two personae at once. An English gentleman will always be perfectly turned out, even in the most difficult times. Happiness in life depends on how we 'filter' reality and interpret it. We can create our own wonderful world. If we don't, we have failed to explore and exploit the power of our own imagination.

ONE HOUR A DAY A COMMIT TO YOUR GOALS

Even if you only fulfil six tasks out of ten, congratulate yourself. We should all do a little more each day – even for five minutes – to bring us closer to our dreams: make a telephone call, write an email or letter, read a few pages of an author whose work you want to get to know. Promise yourself to accomplish one item for pleasure, and another out of obligation. Long-term commitments are difficult to respect (dieting, not complaining, taking exercise). Things we commit to 'for a day' are easier. Or try keeping a 'promise for an hour': do something you've been putting off or dislike, take an hour of physical exercise, do the ironing, sort out your papers and accounts.

Don't worry about what others will think of you – even the most eccentric behaviour will bear fruit. Make time to do something just for yourself. Focus for a quarter of an hour (no more) on a project. Little by little, it will take shape, with no apparent effort.

Five minutes of concentration are worth an hour of scattered but ineffective activity.

VISUALISE YOUR LIFE

The best way to clarify an idea is to visualise it. If you can keep an image in your head for seventeen seconds, it will become a virtual reality. Visualise where and how you will be in a month, or a year, who you may be with, what you'll be wearing, how you'll live the rest of your life, how you would like to die, what you would like people to remember about you. Visualise the person you are inside, what you like about them, what they bring to you. Next, visualise the famous people you most admire, people you've met or would most like to meet. Organise a 'mind conference' and gather them all around you, receive their advice and encouragement. Let them share their secrets with you. Follow in their footsteps. Inside us all is a person full of vitality, energy, charisma. Who will you be when you are ninety years old? What can you do now to become that person? What changes can you make to become healthier, more open, wiser, more cheerful? Most top athletes visualise their competitions in advance. They see themselves winning, receiving accolades, savouring their achievement.

IDENTIFY WHAT YOU CAN INFLUENCE, AND WHAT YOU CAN'T

'Why do you change yourself, then, with things for which you are not accountable? You're merely creating trouble for yourself.'

Epictetus, *Discourses*

If you desire something that you are powerless to obtain, you will be unhappy. Things you can influence and acquire, however, are fully within your grasp.

With each potentially negative experience, ask yourself what qualities you can bring to make use of it or learn from it.

Apply yourself to things you know you can accomplish, or obtain.

A person who depends on others to get what he or she wants is a beggar.

Speak to the things that are not within your power: tell them that they are nothing to you.

The only things we truly 'own' are the uses to which we put our ideas, the things we choose to aspire to, our judgement, our moral qualities, and the work we can do to better ourselves. We are not masters of our destiny: our health, our material wealth, and our social status can take a different course from the one we hope to maintain.

Reading and writing

READ AS MUCH AS YOU CAN

Everything we read enters the fabric of our subconscious. Most writing is based on one person's observations. And so, in the course of an afternoon, we can harvest the fruits of a lifetime of observation, hard work, research, suffering, experience. Take notes while reading to help you remember the essence of a book; extract from your reading the things that touch you personally, and copy them out. This will constitute a living, vibrant portrait of your true nature.

Words and pictures give us moral support, pleasure, vitality and hope.

Read in peace and quiet, without music, coffee or biscuits. After a chapter or a few pages, close the book and think about what you have read.

Words exist to express our thoughts. Once a thought has been assimilated by our subconscious mind, words are no longer needed. But knowledge must precede thought, if we are to attain enhanced self-knowledge. Each of us is a unique collage, of our parents, our friends, our studies, experiences and travels, our reading. We are shaped by innumerable messages: we cannot remember them, but they have changed us, one by one, to a greater or lesser extent.

Sharing our thoughts does not necessarily mean defining limits (through affirmation or denial). A cultivated person can perceive the unity and multiplicity of a thing all at once, and see no contradiction. An open, alert mind is more important than the quality of our comprehension.

Literature is not without risks of its own, however: it can stifle our capacity to experience things for ourselves, and encourage excessive flights of imagination. Often, people are afraid to change their opinions because they are 'possessed' by things they have read. Like material possessions, they do not want to let them go. Too much reading drains our energy. Don't own more books than you can possibly read. Keep just a few authors, a few works, a few texts – but the most important ones for you.

Rather than read too much, alternate your reading with writing, and keep notes on what you have read: this will force you to express your own opinions and ideas clearly and precisely. It will imprint them on your mind, and enable you to draw on them in everyday life.

We make the things we have heard, read or written, our own. They penetrate us, and help us to interpret our experiences.

Reading and writing are, then, forms of self-care. Ideally, we will strike a balance between reading, writing and reflection, like bees buzzing from flower to flower, choosing the blooms that will help them make the finest honey. Keep to one side everything you have 'harvested' in your reading. Apply yourself diligently to collating these multiple finds, to forge a more solid, authentic 'me', an identity that is yours and yours alone.

WRITE TO ASSERT YOUR PERSONALITY

'So rescue yourself from these general themes and write
about what your everyday life offers you; describe your
sorrows and desires, the thoughts that pass through your
mind and your belief in some kind of beauty. Describe all
these with heartfelt, silent, humble sincerity and, when you
express yourself, use the things around you, the images from
your dreams, and the objects that you remember. If your
everyday life seems poor, don't blame it; blame yourself;
admit to yourself that you are not enough of a poet to call
forth its riches; because for the creator there is no poverty
and no poor, indifferent place.'

Rainer Maria Rilke, *Letters to a Young Poet*

If you find yourself at a loss, unable to know what to do, take a sheet of paper and write down everything that is running through your mind. We may lose sight of ideas if our thinking is panicked and muddled, but words can bring meaning and direction. Write down the things you want. The very act of committing them to paper will set a magical process in motion. Practise knowing and expressing exactly what it is you want.

We can only release our thoughts once we have expressed them clearly. Only then can we eliminate them effectively. Writing is a useful way to listen to yourself and achieve self-knowledge. Once you have assimilated an idea as a firm conviction, destroy all your written notes: leave only the impression of the words in your mind. Keep only pleasant things in your notes. In darker times, you will have a storehouse of riches, accomplishments and joys to savour:

proof of the many good things you have experienced, and the many more to come.

To write is to get in touch with your own mind. It's an act that engages the intellect, the intuition and the imagination all at once. If we do not define exactly where we are, how can we choose to take another direction and move on?

Write when you feel angry. This is the best way to put some distance between yourself and your problems – as if, somehow, they are no longer truly yours. This is the best 'sleeping draught' of all. Spill some ink and pour out your heart of hearts – you will feel soothed and serene.

Our internal visualisations are as balmy for the soul as a beautiful natural prospect is for the eyes. To this end, poetry, novels and films are indispensable. Keep your own notebook of quotations, poems, jokes, anecdotes, stories, memories.

WORK YOUR MEMORY

*'Human intelligence should practise the discipline of what
we call idea, moving from a multitude of sensations to a
unity, the gathering of which is an act of reflection. And this
act consists of remembering objects our mind saw in the past,
when it strolled in the company of an immortal god.'*

Racine, *Phèdre*

Remember what's in your head; open the drawers of your memory one by one, recite the things you know by heart, remember foundational phrases you have read. This is the best way to cultivate your memory.

Talk to yourself. Say aloud the names of things, in order to remember them. Memorisation is the best way to acquire experience and wisdom. Top athletes memorise key phrases, for example, then say them regularly so that they are imprinted on the mind. Each day, these phrases dictate physical actions to be accomplished, and the body adopts them without thinking.

INVEST IN KNOWLEDGE

'Zen ... represents human effort to reach through meditation zones of thought beyond the range of verbal expression ... and thus to put oneself in harmony with this absolute ... The intellectual man is a machine ... knowledge is what the mind and spirit assimilate.'

Inazo Nitobe, *Bushido: The Soul of Japan*

Learning is a highly active exercise of the mind, leading to active changes in the body. The body is the physical outcome of everything we have been taught since birth. New knowledge, new learning, new faculties help the body and mind to grow and mature. Don't spend your money on new material possessions, spend it on learning instead. Knowledge is the one thing that can never be taken away. It's an investment whose value can only grow. But beware: don't think of knowledge as a possession. People who have the ability never to think about themselves do not talk about what they know, but rather the ideas they create. They do not depend on the extent of their knowledge. Knowledge is what is assimilated by the mind.

The best way to learn is to teach. Teaching forces you to truly 'own' a subject, to display your knowledge and to work to express it more and more effectively. This forces us to raise our standards of excellence, and to think in creative, articulate ways.

Loosen your consciousness. Accept the irrational and incomprehensible: it will elevate and enrich your personality. Sadly, we in the West are often thwarted in this by our intellectual, moral and religious 'authorities'.

Knowledge is power. But Westerners only take account of things expressed in words. Oriental people, on the other hand, think it pointless to try and express irrational experiences in words.

Exercises and discipline

WHY DO WE NEED EXERCISES?

More than a way to train yourself or acquire knowledge, self-correction is a liberating process.

We need to work on ourselves, to correct our faults and find ways to become what we ought always to have been, but never were.

Exercises of all kinds require first and foremost an ordered, systematic approach, a sequence in time, a moment of the day, a day of the week, a month of the year. But once that first degree of systematic learning has been acquired, we should adjust our exercises to our condition, our age or our energy of the day. The most important thing is to execute them with as much consciousness as possible and not merely mechanically.

Ethics demand practice, consistency, hard work. This is not an obligation, but a personal, existential choice.

Self-discipline is the only true philosophy. We must confront ourselves.

Above all, we should enjoy our exercises, and experience them as a source of enrichment, a necessity. We can all learn to derive aesthetic pleasure and enjoyment from the existence of necessary things: food as a means to satisfy our hunger, drinks to assuage our thirst, and shelter to protect us from bad weather and attacks in the outside world.

Before we begin to practise an exercise, we should be sure it won't become a painful ordeal, and that the pleasure and satisfaction it procures will intensify with our mastery of it over time.

First, determine what you know yourself to be capable of. Next, commit yourself to the exercise for a day, two days, a week. The ideal period is twenty-eight days, after which the body and spirit will have integrated the practice as a habit.

Striking a balance between discipline and letting go, action and repose is difficult but fascinating – it's an exercise that demands constant attention, but without which change is impossible.

EFFECTIVE EXERCISE SECRETS

The secret of the success of any exercise is quantity. Guard against excess (as always!) and you are less likely to fall ill, or be tempted to extremes. An exercise is only beneficial if it is undertaken in a positive, pleasant and fruitful way. Then and only then will it be experienced as a need, and repeated regularly. The body should not encumber the soul, which should remain free and available for intellectual activity, reading, and writing – this is the ultimate aim of taking exercise.

SOME EXERCISES

MORNING EXERCISES

'In the morning when thou risest unwillingly, let this thought be present – I am rising to the work of a human being ... those who love their several arts exhaust themselves in working at them unwashed and without food; but thou valuest thy own nature less than the turner values the turning art, or the dancer the dancing art.'

Marcus Aurelius

First thing each morning, set the programme for your day. Remember the overall aim of everything you do. Tell yourself that you are journeying towards your own perfection. Each new day is a step up in your life. Intimate thoughts such as these are the foundation blocks of the aesthetic of our existence. But avoid straying into narcissism.

DAYTIME EXERCISES

Work to build your physical stamina: your psychological resilience will be enhanced, too, and you will be better able to endure hard times without complaint or collapse. Practise resisting cold, hunger, the urge to sleep. Allow your body just what it needs to function properly. From time to time inflict tough treatment to help you endure life's knocks.

Practise moderation, patience, resist temptation when it presents itself, wait a few moments before opening a letter, a gift.

EVENING EXERCISES

Prepare for your night's sleep by reviewing everything you have done during the day, and by cleansing your thoughts. Refuse to mull over negative thoughts – even for an evening – and you will experience more peaceful sleep.

List the things you have accomplished – remember how you set about them, think about how you might have done them differently, or why you failed to accomplish them, and what conclusions can be drawn from the experience.

Next, complete a purification ritual: breathe a fragrance, a flower, an incense stick; listen to some music, take a bath and prepare yourself for restorative sleep by asking the night to bring repose, and your choice of dreams.

POVERTY, FRUGALITY AND DETACHMENT

'I remember one day, in the Sahara, a Bedouin offered me
sweet tea served in a tiny glass. He had prepared it with
great ceremony, boiling water in an old tin on a little fire
lit from two or three sticks. He had only one glass, so he
prepared my tea first, and when I had finished, he prepared
his own.'

A traveller's memory

For many mystics and thinkers, in the West and East alike, poverty is seen as a virtue. In Zen doctrine, the word 'poverty' doesn't mean simply a lack of money, it refers to humility of the spirit, and the renunciation of temporal desires.

The Scottish thinker and writer Thomas Carlyle undertook a comparative study of poverty and the philosophy of the Void, concluding that we should renounce duality in all its forms. Carlyle followed in the footsteps of the thirteenth- century Dominican monk Meister Eckhart, who dedicated himself to preaching a complete lack of possessions, and an openness to the Void as the only true philosophy of life – a rational, non-realist and nonetheless religious approach. The frugality described in his sermons was not material, but internal.

To want nothing means attaching no importance to the ego (which is not to be confused with self-esteem). Many people have

219

money, but live impoverished lives. They have lost their enthusiasm for life, even their memories of the joys of youth, and for Meister Eckhart, as for Buddhists, the true causes of human misery are acquisitiveness, a hunger for possessions, and an insatiable ego. All great masters have one concept in common: non-attachment.

Our goal is not to have, but to be. Of course, possessing nothing is impossible because this leads to dependence on others. As the German philosopher and psychoanalyst Erick Fromm rightly explains, to look at a flower is to 'be'. To cut it is to 'have'.

Carl Jung argued that Westerners could not understand Buddhism because Western society is centred on ownership and desire. In this sense, Eckhart, too, can be as difficult for Westerners to understand as Zen doctrine, or the poetry of Bashō. The Japanese concept of *sei hin* (*sei* meaning cleanliness, and *hin* meaning beauty) places a higher importance on purity of heart than on material riches. This is why the merchant classes were traditionally viewed with suspicion in Japanese society.

POVERTY

We need only enough to live: adequate financial security to ensure our independence and dignity.

We know, too, that it is more bearable to own little, than to lose everything we have. By detaching ourselves from material possessions, we detach ourselves psychologically and spiritually, too. All this is possible: the easiest person to say 'no' to is . . . you!

And so we can savour the pleasure of leading a pared-down life of true economy.

This deliberate embrace of poverty, backed by simple tastes, can become a source of riches. By adopting this lifestyle we learn, little by little, to evaluate the practical quality of things, rather than their quality as 'badges of worth'. Eating only to satisfy our hunger, mastering ourselves to control feelings of anger; all are necessary if we are to find peace. We have to step outside ourselves, leave ourselves – and all we own – behind.

Paradoxically, anyone who practises self-denial will find that they are able to keep whatever they want, precisely because they have relinquished all the things they did not expressly desire. A person with few possessions is not impoverished, but a person who constantly desires more is. Anyone who embraces a frugal lifestyle is rich.

The deliberate embrace of poverty means leading a simple, sober life: wealth is measured as what is necessary, and what is sufficient.

Epicureanism has its roots in asceticism. No item will benefit its owner if he or she has not first prepared themselves for its loss.

Imagine owning nothing but an apartment, a bed, a table, a computer, a small fitted kitchen and a few clothes. No jewellery, no books, no ornaments . . . Would you be in heaven, or hell?

Practise poverty. Practise abstinence as a regular exercise, one you can return to from time to time, and which will enable you to reshape your life. It's a practise through which you can study detachment from the things around you. We should all deprive ourselves of 'luxuries' from time to time, in order not to suffer if fate robs us of everything one day. We must learn to live very simply, and happily.

Practise poverty so that you will not fear it: if you're in the habit of drinking only the finest quality arabica, try instant coffee once a week.

Blind self-denial is as fundamentally stupid as a luxurious, sophisticated lifestyle. It is also impossible to achieve. We must strive for a happy medium: an equable balance between the urge to seize every opportunity that presents itself, and the option to stand by, arms firmly crossed. Attach yourself only to those things that are of real importance. Always ask yourself whether what you are doing is worthwhile, and what the effect of relinquishing it would be. Ask this of a material possession, a professional engagement, a family decision.

MINIMALISM, ETHICS AND RELIGION

The seemingly empty, hostile desert is home to nomads who possess only things they truly need – not 'possessions' as such, but vital necessities. Be wary of virtue and organised religion, especially if it appears fundamentally lifeless and formal. We do not need to be part of a community to live with compassion and humility. Nor do we achieve simplicity or minimalism by renouncing knowledge and living the life of an illiterate shepherd. On the contrary, simplicity and minimalism are achieved by expanding our awareness of the world and communing with its immensity.

The paths to humility, frank honesty and compassion begin with the way we lead our lives. Why do we always strive to be the best, the wealthiest, the most intelligent? Why do we seek constantly to belittle others with our knowledge, power, money? By living simply, with little, we can abolish injustice, the conformity of conspicuous consumption and poor taste, prejudice and social conventions.

We can live in greater comfort by practising reasonable ascetcism that by surrounding ourselves with unequal, excessive bourgeois luxuries. In ancient Japan, hermits practiced lives of simplicity and poverty that were celebrated as art forms, living in modest homes, eating little, owning little, barely going out in society.

Things accumulated for their own sake are lifeless. We should never accord them greater importance than our life, our time, our energy.

The simple life means more than merely contenting yourself with a frugal meal. It means aspiring to a higher plane of thought, a superior way of life. It means appreciating everything, discovering the joy inherent in the simplest everyday things. It means making the most of everything that comes our way.

Wasteful people lack the ability to live with thankfulness for the things they have: they may own three cars and still feel intensely dissatisfied. So many pleasures come to us free of charge, yet too often we fail to enjoy them: libraries stocked with thousands of books, woods for picnicking, lakes for swimming, instructive radio programmes . . . the true definition of wastefulness is having things we do not enjoy or use. When we have too much, we overlook so many opportunities.

Simplicity requires balance. It means measuring the extent of our appreciation of the material world, and taking effective advantage of the happiness available to us. It means making wise use of our money, time and possessions.

Living 'well' does not mean living in constant self-denial. To live well we must adopt a positive attitude in the face of privation, and not count on material things to make us happy. We all have so many unexplored riches within us.

ENOUGH IS ENOUGH

'A thinking person always has enough.'

Lao Tseu

A plain, sober existence is the most intelligent way of life – simple but elegant. It can be summed up with the magic word 'enough'.

Enough to live, enough to eat, enough to feel content. Finding your personal definition of what 'enough' means is a sure path to happiness.

If you seek to satisfy your each and every need, you will never have 'enough'.

The essential thing is to live with serenity and intensity.

By detaching yourself from things, you can detach yourself from people and their mind-numbing principles. You will become thoroughly adaptable to external things, accepting and receiving everything with joy. When you have abandoned and rejected everything from within, you will be free of attachments. Everything you do can be dictated by circumstance. The ideal is to be attached to nothing and dependent on nobody, happy to act merely out of a humble desire for perfection.

The things we stand to lose are less important than those we stand to gain. We can achieve our goals by focusing on the essential, the beautiful, on perfection.

RENUNCIATION

Detachment is the fruit of renunciation, and renunciation is the first condition if detachment is to be achieved.

Our primary concern should always be a more profound recognition of our inner self, yet we waste time and precious energy accumulating objects and possessions, and seeking pleasure in food, drink and exciting experiences. We strive endlessly for more possessions and time, but we forget that power and knowledge are inside each one of us.

Renunciation is the most difficult thing of all.

To learn renunciation – to relinquish things by choice – we need to set reasonable goals. If we want to journey far, we must start out quietly and pace ourselves, or we will exhaust our reserves. We must learn how to make the best of our mistakes, if we are to progress. Renunciation and detachment are not achieved in a few days, nor merely by offloading our possessions. True renunciation is internal. Our human consciousness needs periods of assimilation and periods of preparation. Many things cannot be assimilated at the first attempt, because they have not become established as a part of our consciousness over time.

'I, me, mine' are chains. They enslave us because they apply to the things that enrich us: wealth, money, power, a name. They are the equivalent of the verbs 'to take', 'to cling on to', to 'want', to 'accumulate'. These are of course typical human tendencies, but to be human also means to seek happiness. Elsewhere. Once you have trained your brain and nervous system to embrace the idea of non-dependence, and to go no further, you will obtain everything you desire in life. And you will look at the world through far more optimistic eyes. 'Practice' and 'training' are the key.

It is vital, in our youth, to savour every pleasure, to own whatever we want, to experiment. Only then can we understand the pleasure in renunciation, and the calm of mind that also comes with it, and not only from the small pleasures of everyday life.

Economise your energy

<hr>

REDISCOVER YOUR NATURAL ENERGY

'The soul, that bright, bluish spark moving at incredible
speed, like electric light ... The yogi was capable of detaching
his soul from his body, from which it came and went as it
pleased.'

Théophile Gautier, *The Romance of the Mummy*

Imagine energy flowing like water through your body. We are encumbered by excess of all kinds. It invades our material and psychological world. Ridding ourselves of this excess does not mean suffering privation, denial, impoverishment. On the contrary, it means creating more space, clarity and lightness. We acquire and expend energy through ideas. Stop making value judgements. Don't place too much importance on things or events. Life's contradictions deplete our powers and bring us pain. Ridding yourself of excess doesn't only mean creating space and saving time. It means limiting the emotional, physical and moral stasis that diminishes us, drains us, and prevents us from taking action. We risk distancing ourselves from essentials, without realising it, because we have too many distractions. We each possess our own vital energy; why, then, do some people feel lacklustre and fatigued? The fact is, we are all gifted with essential, human energy, but our daily lives are so busy, we no longer feel its presence. The air around us is charged with electricity. Machines produce and distribute electricity. And human life is driven by an electric current of a kind – the vital

227

energy known to the Chinese as qi. This is the energy that drives our actions, thoughts and life. Everything – material objects, people, art, our clothes, our food – affects our qi. Each individual life is a series of sensations, a tradition and chain of past thoughts that are as real a source of energy in the mind as electricity in the world of physics. The elements of our personal make-up dictate the way we lead our life. Each individual is the projection of a host of different expressions and activities. Each of us is activated by the quality of the matter from which we are made. But matter is driven by the mind. Modern molecular and material science only confirm what the Orient has always known: that the world is an illusion. In China, Taoism uses qi to attain higher levels of physical and spiritual energy. We know that our state of mind can alter the way our bodies function and look. Hence we know, too, that change is possible if we desire it powerfully enough. To make change happen, we must summon and concentrate our psychic energy.

THE HUMAN BODY – A CONDUIT FOR QI

The concept of qi originated in China. It was discovered by Taoists studying the teachings and mysteries of the Yellow Emperor and Lao Tse. Researchers in all fields – medicine, religion, psychology, philosophy, physics – are drawn to the study of our relationship with the universe. Modern physics recognises that everything in the universe is expressible as pulsating energy, randomly constituted and concretised as matter at particular moments.

In this sense, matter is merely the material expression of patterns and densities of energy. Everything on Earth, from mobile phones to ocean waves, or our own nervous system, is a part of the global energy we refer to as 'life'. Alternative medicine (acupuncture, homeopathy, biofeedback, therapeutic massage) accesses these electric, magnetic, mental and psychic energy fields, operating beyond the random boundaries of our own bodies.

We are an immense sum of restless energy. This is why Oriental thinkers have always maintained the need to restore the natural pulsating energies that are the essence of our being. We fight one another, flee, and surrender. In other words, we can expand or contract our energy, like reptiles. When everyday difficulties, anger and frustration rob us of our energy, we must act to heal our thoughts and emotions and understand their importance. Virtually all maladies can be cured in this way, and certain miracles explained, provided we learn to live in the present moment. Faith, liberation and joyfulness are essential.

CONTROL YOUR ENERGY

'Don't think of someone as a body, but as
a current of living energy.'

Mishima

Reach out to the things that bring you satisfaction, personal enrichment and liberation. We know instinctively which activities, things, ideas and thoughts we associate with these qualities. If we define clearly what we want, and why we want it, we can listen to the small inner voice that is our guide. This is why thinking and dreaming about the things we desire is good for us. We can talk for hours on a subject we feel passionate about, and never feel tired. Our favourite topics fascinate and inspire us. They help us to feel more 'ourselves'. They are a source of the energy we call 'joy', or 'enthusiasm'. In esoterism there is no such thing as blind faith, only knowledge. We are born with mental faculties and a body that develop throughout life, elevating the powers within us.

We perceive reality through the mind only. Its power is limitless. When we gather our mental forces, the mind is capable of controlling and overreaching matter. For this, our body must be in peak condition – it is the mind's ally in the effort to access greater reserves of energy.

SAVE YOUR ENERGY

An overworked mind is associated with an unhealthy body. If you do not live simply and frugally, if you do not keep your body supple and stress-free, if you fail to respect others, or the natural world, your health will suffer. You will find it difficult to control your anxiety and lead a happy, contented life. Ideas that do not become deeply held convictions will have no impact. And convictions come with experience. Indian Ayurvedic medicine is rooted in the conviction that the mind exerts a powerful influence over the body: the absence of disease depends on our degree of psychic awareness, and the balance we strive to maintain.

QI AND ENTHUSIASM

Discard negative thoughts and concentrate your energies on what you truly want to be or have. 2,600 years ago, Lao Tseu stated that the human body is composed of tiny particles held together by energy. He believed the mind was an agent acting upon the body in mysterious ways, and keeping it alive. Lao Tseu recommended we nourish our qi and seek to increase our vital energies. Do not cultivate a taste for sorrowful things, he wrote, even if they are beautiful. Ancient Chinese culture had no concept of 'lively' or 'sad' music, or that certain harmonies and types of music could engender specific emotions. Music was a means of treatment and spiritual elevation.

Enthusiasm is an emotion that spurs us into action. It is a powerful energy form, to be cultivated with dedication. But how can we feel enthusiasm if our body is sick? Healthy people are bright and cheerful; they enjoy life and its pleasures. One secret to achieving this is to bring to mind, as vividly as possible, the very best moments of your life – moments that have transported you to a higher plane. Have you ever felt sad for no particular reason, and then received a call from a friend, inviting you on an outing? Your melancholy is instantly forgotten. Life rushes in at that moment. Choose your friends, your music, your reading, with great care. Contemporary society has become too passive: we accept whatever the radio, TV, social media or fashion imposes on us.

One thing alone is true: live well. But to live well we must be truly 'alive', and love life itself.

QI IN EVERYDAY LIFE

The transformation of the body is essential if it is to be purified and its essence preserved. To do this, we must maintain clear, untrammelled channels of transmission. Impure blood is the root of most illnesses. Foodstuffs contribute their own energy, too. 'Dead' foods lead to death. Too much food blocks our energy. Remain active, walk, take massages, meditate, breathe deeply. Don't neglect insomnia: sleeping pills are a palliative, not the cure. Our nervous system may have suffered irremediable damage, but failing that, we must look elsewhere to find the cause of our lack of sleep. Without proper sleep, or a few hours of deep, restorative sleep at the very least, we cannot live well. Insomnia is often due to blocked qi: if our qi is prevented from circulating freely, it forms knots, directing too much energy to certain parts of the body, and especially the brain, which becomes overactive and cannot rest. Practising certain forms of yoga, and walking, can help spread the qi more evenly throughout the body. Water is also crucially important for the qi. Before a storm, positive ions multiply in the air, which is laden with water, creating the familiar sensation of tension or fatigue. Once the storm has broken, we feel an immediate sense of relief. Negative ions, in plentiful supply around large stretches of moving water (on riverbanks, in tumbling streams, torrents or cascades), are precious sources of renewed qi. The Chinese believe that water is a sacred bearer of vital energy.

In conclusion

TRAVEL, LIVE LIFE TO THE FULL

'So long as people continue to travel to distant, secluded villages where they can find a small room in which to spend the night; so long as they continue to enjoy public transport and street traders that change with the seasons, they will find comfort in small things.'

Alexandra David-Néel, *My Journey to Lhasa*

Sedentary occupations lead to nervous depression, poor quality of life and dissolution. Allow light, positive, pleasant thoughts to penetrate the darkest corners of your mind. Try to reinterpret your past in a positive light, and don't ponder your life here on Earth. It is a question without an answer. Ask instead what life expects of you. Take a change of scene, seek new faces and climates. Travelling refreshes the mind and the morale, it relaxes, relieves and regenerates the spirit.

How can we be free if we cling to home like an oyster to a rock, mired in routine and boredom? Travel for pleasure – not to return home with expensive trophies or a head full of prejudices and unfavourable comparisons. A pencil and notebook are all we need. Many people fear instability. Others hate fixed, unchanging situations. Still others dread that tomorrow will be exactly like today. But a pathway can be fascinating and alluring precisely because we have no idea where it leads. Setting out for an unknown destination, with no ties or obligations, minimal luggage, and the world at your feet is a joy! Find satisfaction in the simple fact of being there, with nothing and nobody, carried along by the charm of the landscape and new faces. The experience will leave an indelible trace in your soul.

LAUGH AND BE HAPPY

Laughter is essential. It empties our heads and hearts; it is a cleansing force. Certain Indian hospitals prescribe it as a treatment for patients. Laughter relaxes and unlines the face, helping emotions of all kinds to rise to the surface. People who laugh are seldom ill.

Concentrate on the here and now: it is rich enough. Tell yourself that all things change, even troubles and unhappiness. Nothing is immutable.

Draw up a list of the things that give you pleasure. Try to satisfy at least one pleasure each day. Do some gardening or cooking, go for a walk, drink tea with a couple of slices of toast. Create something you can admire later (a tray of freshly baked biscuits, a well-tended garden, a perfectly tidy and well-organised cupboard). Happiness depends on the smallest of things: we should never give up trying to be free, modest, pleasant and sociable. Happiness is a continual struggle, a physical exercise to be practised at every moment. We need to know how to defend ourselves against all comers, how to create our own protective shell. We need to know that wherever it is possible to live, it is also possible to live well.

Do not make ephemeral goods your goal. Instead, find ultimate, lasting happiness in your mind and spirit. Be free, and create your own aesthetic of existence.

Everything can make us happy. With each moment of happiness, we feel more complete, and better able to help ourselves. We become our own selves. Many small aspects of everyday life can be sources of happiness: writing to a loved one, planning a meal with friends, tidying a cupboard.

Do you have dreams for the future? They are a sure sign that you continue to believe in yourself. As long as we stay alive, we have choices. People who convince themselves that they are poor or unhappy fail to cultivate their imagination and allow the many potentially beautiful or profound things they have inside to wither and die.

FIND INNER TRANQUILLITY

'Whoever believes himself to be happy, is happy.
Everything I have is within me.'

Stilpo of Megara, third century BC, a disciple of Socrates

No one will ever find greater tranquillity or retreat than in his or her own heart of hearts, that fount of ideas and concepts upon which we have only to focus to find instant peace and perfect order.

PREPARE FOR THE WORST,
ACCEPT LIFE AND SMILE

Accept the inevitable with grace, and tell yourself that the experience will be helpful, somehow. Avoid whatever can be avoided, and face the rest steadfastly and patiently.

Accepting the worst in our own mind helps to eliminate doubts, false hopes, and anxiety. When we tell ourselves that we have everything to lose, we will certainly gain something, too. A failure to accept life as it is prevents us from growing and moving on. We are our own disciple and master over the course of a single day. Wisdom consists in knowing what to do at a given moment. When we stop resisting the inevitable, we can live richer lives.

Don't try to banish misfortune. Accept it, and look for beauty and compensating factors wherever you are. Get up early, and take a little exercise – like elderly people all over China, practising qi gong in the city parks. Live by your own nature, in harmony with the seasons.

LIFE AND DEATH

'The important thing is not to live, but to live well.'

Plato, *Crito*

Only when we relish life are we truly alive. A recognition of life's 'brief candle' (in Shakespeare's words) encourages us to make the most of our existence, and to live consciously, mindfully, truly, and always with a sense of our own limitations. This brings peace of mind. It helps us to accept the worst and release our energy. Our time on Earth is limited: we owe it to ourselves to live as happily as we can in our given circumstances.

Take one step, then another, but don't look too far ahead, or too far behind. Life is a simple matter of eating, sleeping and filling our time as best we can. No one should aspire to be anything more than his or her own self. Often, we ask too many questions about the meaning of life, then realise that the answer lies not in words, but in those moments when we forget the question! Our aims and ambitions are mere substitutes, sublimations of the sense of being alive. At each stage of our spiritual development, our body is our best ally. The more an individual's life is filled with spirituality, the better they will know how to live in the present moment, and the more fully they will live in their own body. Experience a premonition of the unknown, understand that the universe is filled with mysteries and unexplained phenomena: these are the answers to our questions about the meaning of life. We have to accept a certain 'madness' in order to live – not to seek causality, but to recognise and accept the presence of mystery. As Henry Miller once said, no one who has enjoyed a good dream complains that they were wasting their time. Rather, we are happy to have partaken of an experience that has embellished and elevated our reality.

Beginning in the nineteenth century, Westerners began to confuse the mind and the intellect, seeing no difference between the mind and the soul. The soul needs pleasure, just as the mind needs ideas and the body needs food. Drink champagne, study New Age philosophy and live each moment as if it were your last. We can only be happy if our natural instincts are properly satisfied. Take life one day at a time, follow the winding paths dictated by the binary rhythm of day and night, and the seasons. Love humanity in all its infinite diversity.

The shiny bubbles of false happiness burst when we experience the pain of loss. Living in true happiness means seeking to come close to perfection. Take care of your health and strive to maintain a balance between the intellect and the emotions. Little by little, loss and death will seem no more or less important than the things we have gained, or than life itself. Living is an art that reaches its peak when man no longer needs to work. In our own lifetimes, we will see more and more people living to be 100, 105, 110. And so we must prepare for those wonderful years, gathering together the necessary conditions for a full life. Do not abandon your dreams, or close your mind to mystery. To be happy, live simply.

THESE PAGES ARE FOR YOUR OWN NOTES

*Take pleasure in keeping a list of affirmations, challenges,
advice, needs and circumstances. These words will be a
comfort to carry with you whenever you need them.*